5th Workshop on Indian Language Data: Resources and Evaluation (WILDRE5)

Marseille, France
11-16 May 2020

Editors:

Girish Nath Jha
Kalika Bali
Sobha L

S. S. Agrawal
Atul Kr. Oj

ISBN: 978-1-7138-1280-7

Printed from e-media with permission by:

Curran Associates, Inc.
57 Morehouse Lane
Red Hook, NY 12571

Some format issues inherent in the e-media version may also appear in this print version.

Printed with permission by Curran Associates, Inc. (2020)

For permission requests, please contact the Association for Computational Linguistics
at the address below.

Association for Computational Linguistics
209 N. Eighth Street
Stroudsburg, Pennsylvania 18360

Phone: 1-570-476-8006
Fax: 1-570-476-0860

acl@aclweb.org

Additional copies of this publication are available from:

Curran Associates, Inc.
57 Morehouse Lane
Red Hook, NY 12571 USA
Phone: 845-758-0400
Fax: 845-758-2633
Email: curran@proceedings.com
Web: www.proceedings.com

LREC 2020 Workshop
Language Resources and Evaluation Conference
11–16 May 2020

WILDRE5– 5th Workshop on Indian Language Data: Resources and Evaluation

PROCEEDINGS

Editors:
Girish Nath Jha, Kalika Bali, Sobha L, S. S. Agrawal, Atul Kr. Ojha

Proceedings of the LREC 2020
WILDRE5– 5th Workshop on Indian Language Data: Resources and Evaluation

Edited by: Girish Nath Jha, Kalika Bali, Sobha L, S. S. Agrawal, Atul Kr. Ojha

For more information:
European Language Resources Association (ELRA)
9 rue des Cordelières
75013, Paris
France
http://www.elra.info
Email: lrec@elda.org

Introduction

WILDRE – the 5th Workshop on Indian Language Data: Resources and Evaluation is being organized in Marseille, France on May 16th, 2020 under the LREC platform. India has a huge linguistic diversity and has seen concerted efforts from the Indian government and industry towards developing language resources. European Language Resource Association (ELRA) and its associate organizations have been very active and successful in addressing the challenges and opportunities related to language resource creation and evaluation. It is, therefore, a great opportunity for resource creators of Indian languages to showcase their work on this platform and also to interact and learn from those involved in similar initiatives all over the world.

The broader objectives of the 5th WILDRE will be

- to map the status of Indian Language Resources

- to investigate challenges related to creating and sharing various levels of language resources

- to promote a dialogue between language resource developers and users

- to provide an opportunity for researchers from India to collaborate with researchers from other parts of the world

The call for papers received a good response from the Indian language technology community. Out of nineteen full papers received for review, we selected one paper for oral, four for short oral and seven for a poster presentation.

Workshops Chairs

Girish Nath Jha, Jawaharlal Nehru University, India
Kalika Bali, Microsoft Research India Lab, Bangalore
Sobha L, AU-KBC, Anna University
S. S. Agrawal, KIIT, Gurgaon, India

Workshop Manager

Atul Kr. Ojha, Charles University, Prague, Czech Republic & Panlingua Language Processing
LLP, India

Editors

Girish Nath Jha, Jawaharlal Nehru University, India
Kalika Bali, Microsoft Research India Lab, Bangalore
Sobha L, AU-KBC, Anna University
S. S. Agrawal, KIIT, Gurgaon, India
Atul Kr. Ojha, Charles University, Prague, Czech Republic & Panlingua Language Processing
LLP, India

Ritesh Kumar, Agra University
Shantipriya Parida, Idiap Research Institute, Switzerland
S.K. Shrivastava, Head, TDIL, MEITY, Govt of India
S.S. Agrawal, KIIT, Gurgaon, India
Sachin Kumar, EZDI, Ahmedabad
Santanu Chaudhury, Director, IIT Jodhpur
Shivaji Bandhopadhyay, Director, NIT, Silchar
Sobha L, AU-KBC Research Centre, Anna University
Stelios Piperidis, ILSP, Greece
Subhash Chandra, Delhi University
Swaran Lata, Retired Head, TDIL, MCIT, Govt of India
Virach Sornlertlamvanich, Thammasat University, Bangkok, Thailand
Vishal Goyal, Punjabi University, Patiala
Zygmunt Vetulani, Adam Mickiewicz University, Poland

Table of Contents

Workshop Program

Saturday, May 16, 2020

14:00–	**Inaugural session**
14:45	

14:00–	*Welcome by Workshop Chairs*
14:05	

14:05–	*Inaugural Address*
14:25	

14:25–	*Keynote Lecture*
14:45	

14:45–	**Paper Session**
16:15	

Part-of-Speech Annotation Challenges in Marathi
Gajanan Rane, Nilesh Joshi, Geetanjali Rane, Hanumant Redkar, Malhar Kulkarni and Pushpak Bhattacharyya

A Dataset for Troll Classification of TamilMemes
Shardul Suryawanshi, Bharathi Raja Chakravarthi, Pranav Verma, Mihael Arcan, John Philip McCrae and Paul Buitelaar

OdiEnCorp 2.0: Odia-English Parallel Corpus for Machine Translation
Shantipriya Parida, Satya Ranjan Dash, Ondřej Bojar, Petr Motlicek, Priyanka Pattnaik and Debasish Kumar Mallick

Handling Noun-Noun Coreference in Tamil
Vijay Sundar Ram and Sobha Lalitha Devi

Malayalam Speech Corpus: Design and Development for Dravidian Language
Lekshmi K R, Jithesh V S and Elizabeth Sherly

16:15–	*Break*
16:25	

16:25–
17:45   **Poster Session**

Multilingual Neural Machine Translation involving Indian Languages
Pulkit Madaan and Fatiha Sadat

Universal Dependency Treebanks for Low-Resource Indian Languages: The Case of Bhojpuri
Atul Kr. Ojha and Daniel Zeman

A Fully Expanded Dependency Treebank for Telugu
Sneha Nallani, Manish Shrivastava and Dipti Sharma

Determination of Idiomatic Sentences in Paragraphs Using Statement Classification and Generalization of Grammar Rules
Naziya Shaikh

Polish Lexicon-Grammar Development Methodology as an Example for Application to other Languages
Zygmunt Vetulani and Grażyna Vetulani

Abstractive Text Summarization for Sanskrit Prose: A Study of Methods and Approaches
Shagun Sinha and Girish Jha

A Deeper Study on Features for Named Entity Recognition
Malarkodi C S and Sobha Lalitha Devi

17:45–
18:30   ***Panel discussion***

18:30–18:40	**Valedictory Address**
18:40–18:45	*Vote of Thanks*

Proceedings of the WILDRE5– 5th Workshop on Indian Language Data: Resources and Evaluation, pages 1–6
Language Resources and Evaluation Conference (LREC 2020), Marseille, 11–16 May 2020
© European Language Resources Association (ELRA), licensed under CC-BY-NC

Part-of-Speech Annotation Challenges in Marathi

Gajanan Rane, Nilesh Joshi, Geetanjali Rane, Hanumant Redkar,
Malhar Kulkarni and Pushpak Bhattacharyya
Center For Indian Language Technology
Indian Institute of Technology Bombay, Mumbai, India
{gkrane45, joshinilesh60, geetanjaleerane, hanumantredkar,
malharku and pushpakbh}@gmail.com

Abstract

Part of Speech (POS) annotation is a significant challenge in natural language processing. The paper discusses issues and challenges faced in the process of POS annotation of the Marathi data from four domains *viz.*, tourism, health, entertainment and agriculture. During POS annotation, a lot of issues were encountered. Some of the major ones are discussed in detail in this paper. Also, the two approaches *viz.*, the lexical (L approach) and the functional (F approach) of POS tagging have been discussed and presented with examples. Further, some ambiguous cases in POS annotation are presented in the paper.

Keywords: Marathi, POS Annotation, POS Tagging, Lexical, Functional, Marathi POS Tagset, ILCI

1 Introduction

In any natural language, Part of Speech (POS) such as noun, pronoun, adjective, verb, adverb, demonstrative, etc., forms an integral building block of a sentence structure. POS tagging[1] is one of the major activities in Natural Language Processing (NLP). In corpus linguistics, POS tagging is the process of marking/annotating a word in a text/corpus which corresponds to a particular POS. The annotation is done based on its definition and its context i.e., its relationship with adjacent and related words in a phrase, sentence, or paragraph. A simplified form of this is commonly taught to school-age children, in the identification of words as nouns, verbs, adjectives, adverbs, etc. The term 'Part-of-Speech Tagging' is also known as POS tagging, POST, POS annotation, grammatical tagging or word-category disambiguation.

In this paper, the challenges and issues in POS tagging with special reference to Marathi[2] have been presented. The Marathi language is one of the major languages of India. It belongs to the Indo-Aryan Language family with about 71,936,894 users[3]. It is predominantly spoken in the state of Maharashtra in Western India (Chaudhari et. al., 2017). In recent years many research institutions and organizations are involved in developing the lexical resources for Marathi for NLP activities. Marathi Wordnet is one such lexical resource developed at IIT Bombay (Popale and Bhattacharyya, 2017).

The paper is organized as follows: Section 2 introduces POS annotation; section 3 provides information on Marathi annotated corpora; section 4 describes Marathi tag set; section 5 explains tagging approaches, section 6 presents ambiguous behaviors of the Marathi words, section 7 presents a discussion on special cases, and section 8 concludes the paper with future work.

2 Parts-Of-Speech Annotation

In NLP pipeline POS tagging is an important activity which forms the base of various language processing applications. Annotating a text with POS tags is a standard low-level text pre-processing step before moving to higher levels in the pipeline like chunking, dependency parsing, etc. (Bhattacharyya, 2015). Identification of the parts of speech such as nouns, verbs, adjectives, adverbs for each word (token) of the sentence helps in analyzing the role of each word in a sentence (Jurafsky D. et. al., 2016). It represents a token level annotation wherein it assigns a token with POS category.

3 Marathi Annotated Corpora

Aim of POS tagging is to create a large annotated corpora for natural language processing, speech recognition and other related applications. Annotated corpora serve as an important resource in NLP activities. It proves to be a basic building block for constructing statistical models for the automatic processing of natural languages. The significance of large annotated corpora is widely appreciated by researchers and application developers. Various research institutes in India viz., IIT Bombay[4], IIIT Hyderabad[5], JNU New Delhi[6], and other institutes have developed a large corpus of POS tagged data. In Marathi, there is around 100k annotated data developed as a part of Indian Languages Corpora Initiative (ILCI)[7] project funded by MeitY[8], New Delhi. This ILCI corpus consists of four domains viz., Tourism, Health, Agriculture, and Entertainment. This tagged data (Tourism - 25K, Health - 25K, Agriculture - 10K, Entertainment - 10K, General – 30K) is used for various applications like chunking, dependency tree banking, word sense disambiguation, etc. This ILCI

---

[1]http://language.worldofcomputing.net/pos-tagging/parts-of-speech-tagging.html
[2]http://www.indianmirror.com/languages/marathi-language.html
[3]http://www.censusindia.gov.in/

[4]http://www.cfilt.iitb.ac.in/
[5]https://ltrc.iiit.ac.in/
[6]https://www.jnu.ac.in/
[7]http://sanskrit.jnu.ac.in/ilci/index.jsp
[8]https://meity.gov.in/

annotated data forms a baseline for Marathi POS tagging and is available for download at TDIL portal[9].

4 The Marathi POS Tag-Set

The Bureau of Indian Standards (BIS)[10] has come up with a standard set of tags for annotating data for Indian languages. This tag-set is prepared for Hindi under the guidance of BIS. The BIS tag-set aims to ensure standardization in the POS tagging across the Indian languages. The tag sets of all Indian languages have been drafted by Dept. of Information Technology, MeitY and presented as Unified POS standard in Indian languages[11]. Marathi POS tag-set has been prepared at IIT Bombay referring to the standard BIS POS Tag-set, IIIT Hyderabad guideline document (Bharati et al, 2006) and Konkani Tag-set (Vaz et. al., 2012). This Marathi POS Tag-set can be seen in Appendix A.

5 Lexical and Functional POS Tagging: Challenges and Discussions

Lexical POS tagging (Lexical or L approach) deals with tagging of a word at a token level. Functional POS tagging (Functional or F approach) deals with tagging of a word as a syntactic function of a word in a sentence. In other words, a word can have two roles viz., grammatical role (lexical POS w.r.t. a dictionary entry) and functional role (contextual POS)[12]. For example, in the phrase 'golf stick', the POS tag of the word 'golf' could be determined as follows:

- Lexically it is a noun as per lexicon.
- Functionally it is an adjective as it is a modifier of succeeding noun.

In the initial stage of ILCI data annotation, POS tagging was conducted using the lexical approach. However, over a while, POS tagging was done using the functional approach only. The reason is that, by using the lexical approach we do a general tagging, i.e., tagging at a surface level or token level and by using the functional approach we do a specific tagging, i.e., tagging at a semantic level. This eases the annotation process of chunking and parsing in the NLP pipeline.

While performing POS annotation, many issues and challenges were encountered, some of which are discussed below. Table 1 lists the occurrences of discussed words in the ILCI corpus.

5.1 Subordinators which act as Adverbs

There are three basic types of adverbs. They are time (N_NST), place (N_NST) and manner (RB). Traditionally, adverbs should be tagged as RB. Subordinators are conjunctions which are tagged as CCS.

However, there are some subordinators in Marathi which act as adverbs. For example, ज्याप्रमाणे (*jyApramANe*, like-

wise), त्याप्रमाणे (*tyApramANe*, like that), ह्याप्रमाणे (*hyApramANe*, like this), जेव्हा (*jevhA*, when) and तेव्हा (*tevhA*, then). ज्याप्रमाणे (*jyApramANe*) and त्याप्रमाणे (*tyApramANe*) are generated from pronominal stems viz., ज्या (*jyA*) and ह्या (*hyA*) hence they are lexically qualified as pronouns, however, they function as adverbs; hence to be functionally tagged as RB at the individual level. However, when these words appear as part of the clause then they should be functionally tagged as CCS.

This distinction was also observed by noted Marathi grammarian, Damle[13] (Damle, 1965) [p. 206-07].

5.2 Words with Suffixes

There are suffixes like मुळे (*muLe*, because of; due to), साठी (*sAThI*, for), बरोबर, (*barobara*, along with), etc. When these suffixes are attached to pronouns they function as adverbs or conjunctions at a syntactic level. For example, words त्यामुळे (*tyAmuLe*, because of that), यामुळे (*yAmuLe*, because of this), यासाठी (*yAsAThI*, for this), ह्यामुळे (*hyAmuLe*, because of this), ह्याच्यामुळे (*hyAchyAmuLe*, because of it/him), यांच्यामुळे (*yAMchyAmuLe*, because of them), त्याचबरोबर (=तसेच) (*tyAchabarobara* (=*tasecha*), further) are formed by attaching the above suffixes to pronouns. These words which are formed are lexically tagged as PRP. However, functionally these words act as conjunctions at the sentence level; therefore, they should be tagged as CCD. Also, consider the words त्यावेळी (*tyAveLI*, at that time), ह्यावेळी (*hyAveLI*, at this time), ह्यानंतर (*hyAnaMtara*, after this), त्यानंतर (*tyAnaMtara*, after that). Here, wherever the first string/morpheme appears as त्या (*tyA*) and ह्या (*hyA*), the tag should be given as PRP, lexically. But functionally, all these words shall be tagged as N_NST (time adverb).

5.3 Words which are Adjectives

Adjectives are tagged as JJ. Consider the example below: त्याच्यामध्ये ही कला परंपरागत चालत आली आहे (*tyAchyAmadhye hI kalA paraMparAgata chAlataAllAhe*, this art has come to him by tradition). Lexically, the word परंपरागत (*paraMparAgata*, traditional) is an adjective, but, in the above sentence, it qualifies the verb चालत येणे (*chAlatayeNe*, to be practiced). Hence functionally, the word परंपरागत (*paraMparAgata*) should be tagged as an RB. Similarly, a word वाईट (*vAITa*, bad) has a lexical POS as an adjective (Date-Karve, 1932). But in the sentence मला वाईट वाटते (*malA vAITa vATate*, I am feeling bad), it functions as an adverb, as it is qualifying the verb and not preceding the pronoun मला (*malA*, I; me). Therefore, functionally word वाईट (*vAITa*) acts as adverb hence should be tagged as RB.

5.4 Adnominal Suffixes Attached to Verbs

The adnominal suffix जोगं (*jogaM*) and all its forms (जोगा, जोगी, जोगे, जोग्या; *jogA, jogI, joge, jogyA*) are always attached to verbs. For example, word करण्याजोग्या (*karaNyAjogyA*, doable) is lexically tagged as a verb. However, word करण्या (*karaNyA*) is a Kridanta form of a verb करणे (*karaNe*, to do) and suffix जोगं (*jogaM*) is an adnominal suffix attached to Kridanta form; hence, a verb with all the

---

forms of जोगं (*jogaM*) should functionally be treated as adjectives. Therefore verbs with adnominal suffix should be tagged as JJ.

5.5 Words जसे (*jase*) तसे (*tase*)

As per Damle (1956), words जसे (*jase*, like this) and तसे (*tase*, like that) are tagged as adverbs. However, if they appear with nouns in a sentence, they are influenced by the inflection and gender property of that nominal stem. For example, words जसे (*jase*, like this) and तसे (*tase*, like that) have inflected forms like जसा (*jasA*, like him), जशी (*jashI*, like her), तसा (*tasA*, like this), तशी (*tashI*, like this), तसे (*tase*, like this), etc. All these words function as a relative pronoun in a sentence. Hence, the words and their variations should be functionally tagged as PRL.

5.6 Word तसेतर (*tasetara*)

A word तसेतर (*tasetara*, as it is seen) is the same as तसे पाहिले तर (*tase pAhile tara*, as it is seen). Lexically, it can be tagged as a particle (RPD) but since it has a function of conjunction; it should be tagged as CCD. For example, in a sentence तसेतर तणावामुळेही काळी वलय येतात (*tasetara taNAvAmuLehI kALI valaya yetAta*, as it is seen that black circles appear because of stress as well), word तसेतर (*tasetara*) functions as conjunction and hence should be tagged as CCD instead of tagging it as RPD.

5.7 Word अन्यथा (*anyathA*)

The standard dictionaries give POS of the word अन्यथा (*anyathA*, otherwise; else; or) as an adverb/indeclinable. For example, consider a sentence अन्यथा तो येणार नाही (*anyathA to yeNAra nAhI*, Otherwise, he will not come). Here, while annotating अन्यथा (*anyathA*) there is a possibility that annotator can directly tag this word as an adverb at a lexical level. However, it behaves like conjunction at the sentence level and hence it should be tagged as CCD.

5.8 Different Forms of कसा (*kasA*)

As per BIS Tag-set, words कसा, कशी, कसे (*kasA, kashI, kase*; how) shall be tagged as PRQ. However, the PRQ tag is only for pronoun category and the word कसा (*kasA*) is not a pronoun; it can behave as an adverb or as a modifier. Consider the examples below:

1. तो माणूस कसा आहे हे त्याच्याशी बोलल्यावरच कळेल (*to mANUsa kasA Ahe he tyAchyAshI bolalyAvaracha kaLela*, we will come to know about him only after talking to him) [adnominal]
2. सरकारी ठरावाने कायद्याचे कलम कसे रद्द होणार (*sarakArI TharAvAne kAyadyAche kalama kase radda hoNAra*, How can this clause of law be prohibited by Government Resolution?) [adverbial]

In the 1st case, word कसा (*kasA*, how) functionally acts as a pronoun, hence to be tagged as PRQ. While, in the 2nd case, it acts as an adverb, hence to be functionally tagged as RB.

5.9 Word मात्र (*mAtra*)

A word मात्र (*mAtra*) is very ambiguous in its various usages; it is difficult to functionally identify the POS of this word at a sentence level. Various meanings of word मात्र (*mAtra*) are given in Data-Karve dictionary[14]. Some of the different senses of मात्र (*mAtra*) are discussed here:

- When the word मात्र (*mAtra*) conveys the meaning of ही, देखील, सुद्धा (*hI, dekhIla, suddhA*; also) then it should be tagged as RB functionally.
- When a word is related to the preceding word तेथे (*tethe*, there) and its function is an emphatic marker च (*cha*) then it should be tagged as RPD functionally.
- When word मात्र (*mAtra*) appears in the form of conjunction then it should be marked as CC functionally.
- If the word is modifying the succeeding noun, then it should be tagged as JJ functionally.
- If the word is modifying the preceding word, then the tag will be RPD as a particle functionally.

Therefore, it is noticed that the word मात्र (*mAtra*) does not have one single POS tag functionally and it depends upon the appearance in a sentence. Hence, should be tagged as per the usage.

Token	Lexical	Functional	Occurrences
ज्याप्रमाणे	Pronoun	Adverb	94
त्याप्रमाणे	Pronoun	Adverb	180
ह्याप्रमाणे	Pronoun	Adverb	8
जेव्हा	Subordinator	Time adverb	1496
तेव्हा	Subordinator	Time adverb	1577
मात्र	Adverb	Post-position Conjunction Particle	426
तसेतर	Particle	Conjunction	8
कसा	Wh-word	Adverb	269
त्यामुळे	Pronoun	Conjunction	530
ह्यामुळे	Pronoun	Conjunction	424
ह्याच्यामुळे	Pronoun	Conjunction	8
त्यावेळी	Pronoun	Time adverb	244
ह्यावेळी	Pronoun	Time adverb	33
ह्यानंतर	Pronoun	Time adverb	71
त्यानंतर	Pronoun	Time adverb	298
परंपरागत	Adjective	Adverb	104
वाईट	Adjective	Adverb	246
अन्यथा	Adverb	Conjunction	24
जसे	Relative pronoun	Adverb	1007
तसे	Relative pronoun	Adverb	511
करण्याजोग्या	Verb	Adjective	97

Table 1: Occurrences of discussed words and lexical v/s functional tags assigned to these words

6 POS Ambiguity: Challenges and Discussions

Ambiguity is a major open problem in NLP. Several POS level ambiguity issues were faced by annotators while annotating the Marathi corpus. Following are some POS

---

[14]http://www.transliteral.org/dictionary/mr.kosh.maharashtra/source

specific ambiguity problems encountered while annotating.

6.1 Ambiguous POS: Adjective or Noun?

Examples: वयस्कर (*vayaskara*, the aged)

- कुटुंबाच्या वयस्कर सदस्यांनी मतदान केले (*kuTuMbAchyA vayaskara sadasyAMnI matadAnakele*, all the aged members of the family voted).
- सर्व वयस्करांनी मतदान केले (*sarva vayaskarAMnI matadAna kele*, all the aged people voted).

In the above examples, the word वयस्कर (*vayaskarAMnI*) lexically acts as an adjective as well as a noun. However, at the syntactic level, in the first example, it is functioning as adjective hence to be tagged as JJ, while in the second example it is functioning as a noun hence to be tagged as N_NN. This is one of the challenges while annotating adjectives appearing in nominal form. Annotators usually fail to disambiguate these types of words at the lexical level; therefore such words should be disambiguated at syntactic level. Hence, annotators need to take special care while annotating such cases.

6.2 Ambiguous POS: Demonstrators

While annotating demonstrators such as हा, ही, हे, तो, ती, ते ((*hA, hI, he*), this), (*to, tI, te*), that) annotators often get confused whether to tag them as DMD or DMR. Simple guideline can be followed is, if the demonstrator is directly following noun, then tag it as DMD, otherwise tag it as DMR i.e., if the demonstrator is referring to previous noun/person.

6.3 Ambiguous POS: Noun and Conjunction

Example: word कारण (*kAraNa*, reason; because). At semantic level, the word कारण (*kAraNa*) has two meanings, one is 'a reason' which acts as a noun and another is 'because' which acts as a conjunction. Annotators have to pay special attention while tagging such cases.

6.4 Ambiguous Words: ते (*te*) and तेही (*tehI*)

The word ते (*te*) has different grammatical categories like pronoun (they), demonstrator (that) and conjunction (to). Examples:

- ३० ते ४० (*30 te 40*, 30 to 40)
- The word ते (*te*) lexically and functionally acts as conjunction, hence to be tagged as CCD.
- ते म्हणाले (*te mhaNAle*, they said)
- Here word ते (*te*) acts as personal pronoun, hence to be tagged as PR_PRP
- ते कुठे आहेत? (*te kuThe Aheta?*, where are they?)
- Here word ते (*te*) acts as relative demonstrator, hence to be tagged as DM_DMR
- राकेशने पोलीसांना फोन केला आणि ते दोन्ही चोर पकडले गेले (*rAkeshane polIsAMnA phona kelA ANi te donhI chora pakaDale gele*, Rakesh called police and those two thieves got caught).
- Here, word ते (*te*) is modifying its succeeding noun चोर (*chora*, thief) so it is Deictic demonstrator, hence to be tagged as DM_DMD.

त्यांना हे कधीच पसंत नव्हते, त्यांच्या मुलाने संगीत शिकावे आणि तेही नृत्य (*tyAMnA he kadhIchapasaMtanavhate, tyAMchyAmulAnesaMgItashikAveANitehInRRitya*, He never wanted his son to learn music and that too the dance form)

Here, the word तेही (*tehI*) is an ambiguous word. It is modifying succeeding noun or previous context. Here, ही (*hI*) is a bound morpheme and conveys the meaning 'also'. Therefore word तेही (*tehI*) should be tagged as DM_DMR.

6.5 Ambiguous word: उलटा (*ulaTA*)

Examples:

- उलटे टांगून सुकवले जाते (*ulaTe TAMgUna sukavale jAte*). Here, उलटे (*ulaTe*, upside down is behaving as manner, not a noun, hence to be tagged as RB.
- उलटे भांडे सुलटे कर (*ulaTe bhAMDe sulaTe kara*). Here उलटे (*ulaTe*) it is modifying succeeding noun, hence it is an adjective, hence to be tagged as JJ.

In the above examples, annotator should identify word behavior in the sentence and tag accordingly.

6.6 Ambiguous words: कितीही (*kitIhI*), ना का (*nA kA*) and असू दे ना का (*asU de nA kA*)

Examples:

- संगणक हा कितीही प्रगत किंवा चतुर असू दे ना का, तो केवळ तेच काम करू शकतो ज्याची विधी (पद्धत) आपल्याला स्वत: माहित आहे. (*saMgaNaka hA kitIhI pragata kiMvA chatura asU de nA kA, to kevaLa techa kAma karU shakato jyAchI vidhI (paddhata) ApalyAlA svata: mAhita Ahe*. The computer how much ever may be advanced and clever, it only does that work whose method we only know). Here, कितीही (*kitIhI*, how much) is a quantifier, hence to be tagged as QTF.
- In the phrase असू दे ना का (*asU de nA kA*), the token ना (*nA*) is a part of verb असू दे (*asU de*, let it be) and should be tagged as VM, hence the phrase should be tagged as VM, while the token का (*kA*) is acting as a particle in this phrase and not as a question marker, therefore का (*kA*) should be tagged as RPD.
- किती माणसे जेवायला होती? (*kitI mANase jevAyalA hotI*, how many people were there for a meal?). Here, किती (*kitI*, how many) is a question so it should be tagged as DMQ.

6.7 Ambiguous word: तर (*tara*)

Examples:

- Conjunction: जर मी वेळीच गेलो नसतो तर हा वाचला नसता (*jara mI veLIcha gelo nasato tara hA vAchalA nasatA*, if I had not gone on time he would have not survived).
- Particle: 'हो! आता मी जातो तर!' = 'मी अजिबात जाणार नाही' ('*ho! AtA mI jAto tara!*' = '*mI ajibAta jANA-*

ra nAhI', 'yes! now I am leaving then' = 'I am not at all leaving').

In the above sentences, the word तर (*tara*) is used as a supplementary or stressable word so somewhat special as to give meaning in the sentence. (Date-Karve, 1932). Hence it should be treated as CCD.

- तुम्ही तर लाख रुपये मागतां व मी तर केवळ गरीब पडलो (*tumhI tara lAkha rupaye mAgatAM va mI tara kevaLa garIba paDalo*, you are asking for lakh rupees and I am a poor person). In this sentence, the word तर (*tara*) indicates opposition with respect to meaning between two connected sentences. (Date-Karve, 1932). Hence, it should be treated as a RPD.

7 Discussions on Some Special Cases

- Words आम्लयुक्त (*Amlayukta*), मलईरहित (*malalrahita*), मेदरहित (*medarahita*), दुष्काळग्रस्त (*duShkALagrasta*) are combinations of noun plus adjective suffix such as युक्त (*yukta*), ग्रस्त (*grasta*) and रहित (*rahita*). In such cases, even though noun is a head string and adjective part is a suffix, the whole word shall be tagged as JJ.
- Before tagging अभंग (*abhaMga*, verses), ओव्या (*ovyA*, stanzas), काव्य (*kAvya*, poetry), etc., annotator shall first read between the lines; understand the meaning which it conveys and then decide upon the grammatical categories of each token. For example, in sentence कळवे तयासी कळे अंतरीचे कारण ते साचे साच अंगी (*kaLAve tayAsI kale aMtarIche kAraNa te sAche sAcha aMgI*) the POS tagging should be done as साचे\V_VM साच\N_NN अंगी\N_NN, etc.
- Doubtful cases of word **कोणता** (*koNatA*)

  Examples:

  o कोणता मुलगा हुशार आहे (*koNatA mulagA hushAra Ahe*)?
  o वाहतुकीच्या दरम्यान कोणतीही हानी झालेली नाही (*vAhatukIchyA daramyAna koNatIhI hAnI jhAlelI nAhI*).
  o ह्यांच्या बोलण्याचा माझ्यावर कोणताही परिणाम झाला नाही (*hyAMchyA bolaNyAchA mAjhyAvara koNatAhI pariNAma jhAlA nAhI*).
  o शेतकऱ्यास कोणत्याही वर्षी पाण्याची कमतरता भासणार नाही (*shetakaryAsa koNatyAhI varShI pANyAchI kamataratA bhAsaNAra nAhI*).

  Here, in the 1st example, the word कोणता (*koNatA*, which one) undoubtedly is DMQ. In rest of the examples कोणतीही (*koNatAhI*, whichever, whomever), कोणताही (*koNatAhI*, whichever, whomever), कोणत्याही (*koNatyAhI*, whichever, whomever) are DM adjective (DMD).

8 Conclusion and Future Work

Marathi POS tagging is an important activity for NLP tasks. While tagging, several challenges and issues were encountered. In this paper, Marathi BIS tag-set has been discussed. Lexical and functional tagging approaches were discussed with examples. Further, various challenges, experiences, and special cases have been presented. The issues discussed here will be helpful for annotators, researchers, language learners, etc. of Marathi and other languages.

In future, more issues such as tagging for words having multiple senses; words having multiple functional tags will be discussed. Also, tagset comparison of close languages will be done. Further, the evaluation of lexical and functional tagging using statistical analysis will be done.

References

Akshar Bharati, Dipti Misra Sharma, Lakshmi Bai, Rajeev Sangal. (2006). AnnCorra : Annotating Corpora Guidelines For POS And Chunk Annotation For Indian Languages. *Language Technologies Research Centre*, IIIT, Hyderabad.

Chitra V. Chaudhari, Ashwini V. Khaire, Rashmi R. Murtadak, Komal S. Sirsulla. (2017). Sentiment Analysis in Marathi using Marathi WordNet. *Imperial Journal of Interdisciplinary Research (IJIR)* Vol-3, Issue-4, 2017 ISSN: 2454-1362.

Damle, Moro Keshav. (1965). Shastriya Marathi Vyakran. *A scientific grammar of Marathi,* 3rd edition. Pune, India: RD Yande.

Daniel Jurafsky & James H. Martin. (2016). Speech and Language Processing.

Edna Vaz, Shantaram V. Walawalikar, Dr. Jyoti Pawar, Dr. Madhavi Sardesai. (2012). BIS Annotation Standards With Reference to Konkani Language. *24th International Conference on Computational Linguistics (COLING 2012)*, Mumbai.

Lata Popale and Pushpak Bhattacharyya. (2017). Creating Marathi WordNet. *The WordNet in Indian Languages. Springer*, Singapore, 2017. 147-166.

Pushpak Bhattacharyya, (2015). Machine Translation, *Book published by CRC Press,* Taylor and Francis Group, USA.

Yashwant Ramkrishna Date, Chintman Ganesh Karve, Aba Chandorkar, Chintaman Shankar Datar. (1932). Maharashtra Shabdakosh. *Published by H. A. Bhave, Varada Books,* Senapati Bapat Marg, Pune.

Appendix A

Marathi Parts of Speech Tag-Set with Examples

SI. No	Category	Label	Annotation Convention **	Examples
	Top level & Subtype			
1	**Noun (नाम)**	**N**	**N**	
1.1	Common (जातीवाचक नाम)	NN	N_NN	**गाय**\N_NN **गोठ्यात**\N_NN राहते.
1.2	Proper (व्यक्तीवाचक नाम)	NNP	N_NNP	**रामाने**\N_NNP **रावणाला**\N_NNP मारले.
1.3	Nloc (स्थल-काल)	NST	N_NST	1. तो **येथे**\N_NST काम करत होता. 2. त्याने ही वस्तू **खाली**\N_NST ठेवली आहे.
2	**Pronoun (सर्वनाम)**	**PR**	**PR**	
2.1	Personal (पुरुष वाचक)	PRP	PR_PRP	**मी**\PR_PRP येतो.
2.2	Reflexive (आत्म वाचक)	PRF	PR_PRF	मी **स्वतः**\PR_PRF आलो.
2.3	Relative (संबंधी)	PRL	PR_PRL	**ज्याने**\PR_PRL हे सांगितले त्याने हे काम केले पाहिजे.
2.4	Reciprocal (पारस्परिक)	PRC	PR_PRC	**परस्पर**
2.5	Wh-word (प्रश्नार्थक)	PRQ	PR_PRQ	**कोण**\PR_PRQ येत आहे?
2.6	Indefinite (अनिश्चित)	PRI	PR_PRI	**कोणी**\PR_PRI **कोणास**\PR_PRI हासू नये. त्या पेटीत **काय**\PR_PRI आहे ते सांगा.
3	**Demonstrative (दर्शक)**	**DM**	**DM**	**हे**\DM मुलगी हुशार आहे.
3.1	Deictic	DMD	DM_DMD	**तो**\DM_DMD मुलगा हुशार आहे. **हा**\DM_DMD मुलगा हुशार आहे. **ही**\DM_DMD मुलगी सुंदर आहे. **जेथे**\DM_DMD राम होता **तेथे**\DM_DMD तो होता.
3.2	Relative	DMR	DM_DMR	**हे**\DM_DMR लाल रंगाचे असते.
3.3	Wh-word	DMQ	DM_DMQ	**कोणता**\DM_DMQ मुलगा हुशार आहे?
4	**Verb (क्रियापद)**	**V**	**V**	
4.1	Main (मुख्य क्रियापद)	VM	V_VM	तो घरी **गेला**\V_VM.
4.2	Auxiliary (सहाय्यक क्रियापद)	VAUX	V_VAUX	राम घरी जात **आहे**\V_VAUX.
5	**Adjective (विशेषण)**	**JJ**		**सुंदर**\JJ मुलगी
6	**Adverb (क्रियाविशेषण)**	**RB**		**हळूहळू**\RB चाल.
7	**Conjunction (उभयान्वयी अव्यय)**	**CC**	**CC**	
7.1	Coordinator	CCD	CC_CCD	तो **आणि**\CC_CCD मी.
7.2	Subordinator	CCS	CC_CCS	**जर**\CC_CCS त्याने सांगितले असते **तर**\CC_CCS हे काम मी केले असते.
7.2.1	Quotative	UT	CC_CCS_UT	**असे**\CC_CCS_UT **म्हणून**\C_CCS_UT तो पुढे गेला.
8	**Particles**	**RP**	**RP**	
8.1	Default	RPD	RP_RPD	मी **तर**\RP_RPD खूप दमले.
8.2	Interjection (उद्गार वाचक)	INJ	RP_INJ	**अरेरे**\RP_INJ ! सचिनची विकेट ढापली.
8.3	Intensifier (तीव्र वाचक)	INTF	RP_INTF	राम **खूप**\RP_INTF चांगला मुलगा आहे.
8.4	Negation (नकारात्मक)	NEG	RP_NEG	नको, न
9	**Quantifiers**	**QT**	**QT**	
9.1	General	QTF	QT_QTF	**थोडी**\QT_QTF साखर द्या.
9.2	Cardinals	QTC	QT_QTC	मला **एक**\QT_QTC गोळी दे.
9.3	Ordinals	QTO	QT_QTO	माझा **पहिला**\QT_QTO क्रमांक आला.
10	**Residuals (उर्वरित)**	**RD**	**RD**	
10.1	Foreign word	RDF	RD_RDF	
10.2	Symbol	SYM	RD_SYE	$, &, *, (,),
10.3	Punctuation	PUNC	RD_PUNC	. (period), ,(comma), ;(semi-colon), !(exclamation),? (question), : (colon), etc.
10.4	Unknown	UNK	RD_UNK	Not able to identify the Tag.
10.5	Echo-words	ECH	RD_ECH	जेवण बिवण, डोके बिके

Proceedings of the WILDRE5– 5th Workshop on Indian Language Data: Resources and Evaluation, pages 7–13
Language Resources and Evaluation Conference (LREC 2020), Marseille, 11–16 May 2020
© European Language Resources Association (ELRA), licensed under CC-BY-NC

A Dataset for Troll Classification of TamilMemes

Shardul Suryawanshi[1], Bharathi Raja Chakravarthi[1], Pranav Varma[2],
Mihael Arcan[1], John P. McCrae[1] and Paul Buitelaar [1]
[1] Insight SFI Research Centre for Data Analytics
[1]Data Science Institute, National University of Ireland Galway
[2]National University of Ireland Galway
{shardul.suryawanshi, bharathi.raja}@insight-centre.org

Abstract

Social media are interactive platforms that facilitate the creation or sharing of information, ideas or other forms of expression among people. This exchange is not free from offensive, trolling or malicious contents targeting users or communities. One way of trolling is by making memes, which in most cases combines an image with a concept or catchphrase. The challenge of dealing with memes is that they are region-specific and their meaning is often obscured in humour or sarcasm. To facilitate the computational modelling of trolling in the memes for Indian languages, we created a meme dataset for Tamil (TamilMemes). We annotated and released the dataset containing suspected trolls and not-troll memes. In this paper, we use the a image classification to address the difficulties involved in the classification of troll memes with the existing methods. We found that the identification of a troll meme with such an image classifier is not feasible which has been corroborated with precision, recall and F1-score.

Keywords: Tamil dataset, memes classification, trolling, Indian language data

1. Introduction

Traditional media content distribution channels such as television, radio or newspapers are monitored and scrutinized for their content. Nevertheless, social media platforms on the Internet opened the door for people to contribute, leave a comment on existing content without any moderation. Although most of the time, the internet users are harmless, some produce offensive content due to anonymity and freedom provided by social networks. Due to this freedom, people are becoming creative in their jokes by making memes. Although memes are meant to be humorous, sometimes it becomes threatening and offensive to specific people or community.

On the Internet, a troll is a person who upsets or starts a hatred towards people or community. Trolling is the activity of posting a message via social media that is intended to be offensive, provocative, or menacing to distract which often has a digressive or off-topic content with the intent of provoking the audience (Bishop, 2013; Bishop, 2014; Mojica de la Vega and Ng, 2018; Suryawanshi et al., 2020). Despite this growing body of research in natural language processing, identifying trolling in memes has yet to be investigated. One way to understand how meme varies from other image posts was studied by Wang and Wen (2015). According to the authors, memes combine two images or are a combination of an image and a witty, catchy or sarcastic text. In this work, we treat this task as an image classification problem.

Due to the large population in India, the issue has emerged in the context of recent events. There have been several threats towards people or communities from memes. This is a serious threat which shames people or spreads hatred towards people or a particular community (Kumar et al., 2018; Rani et al., 2020; Suryawanshi et al., 2020). There have been several studies on moderating trolling, however, for a social media administrator memes are hard to monitor as they are region-specific. Furthermore, their meaning is

often obscure due to fused image-text representation. The content in Indian memes might be written in English, in a native language (native or foreign script), or in a mixture of languages and scripts (Ranjan et al., 2016; Chakravarthi et al., 2018; Jose et al., 2020; Priyadharshini et al., 2020; Chakravarthi et al., 2020a; Chakravarthi et al., 2020b). This adds another challenge to the meme classification problem.

(a) Example 1

(b) Example 2

Figure 1: Examples of Indian memes.

In Figure 1, Example 1 is written in Tamil with two images and Example 2 is written in English and Tamil (Roman Script) with two images. In the first example, the meme is trolling about the *"Vim dis-washer"* soap. The information in Example 1 can be translated into English as *"the price of a lemon is five Rupees"*, whereby the image below shows a crying person. Just after the crying person the text says *"The price of a Vim bar with the power of 100 Lemon is just 10 Rupees"*. This is an example of opinion manipulation with trolling as it influences the user opinion about products, companies and politics. This kind of memes might be effective in two ways. On the one hand, it is easy for companies and political parties to gain popularity. On the other hand, the trolls can damage the reputation of the company name or political party name. Example 2 shows a funny meme; it shows that a guy is talking to a poor lady while the girl in the car is looking at them. The image below includes a popular Tamil comedy actor with a short text written beneath *"We also talk nicely to ladies to get into a relationship"*.

Even though there is a widespread culture of memes on the Internet, the research on the classification of memes is not studied well. There are no systematic studies on classifying memes in a troll or not-troll category. In this work, we describe a dataset for classifying memes in such categories. To do this, we have collected a set of original memes from volunteers. We present baseline results using convolutional neural network (CNN) approaches for image classification. We report our findings in precision, recall and F-score and publish the code for this work at *https: //github.com/sharduls007/TamilMemes*.

2. Troll Meme

A troll meme is an implicit image that intents to demean or offend an individual on the Internet. Based on the definition "Trolling is the activity of posting a message via social media that tend to be offensive, provocative, or menacing (Bishop, 2013; Bishop, 2014; Mojica de la Vega and Ng, 2018)". Their main function is to distract the audience with the intent of provoking them. We define troll memes as a meme, which contains offensive text and non-offensive images, offensive images with non-offensive text, sarcastically offensive text with non-offensive images, or sarcastic images with offensive text to provoke, distract, and has a digressive or off-topic content with intend to demean or offend particular people, group or race.

Figure 2 shows examples of trolling memes, Example 3 is trolling the potato chip brand called Lays. The translation of the text is *"If you buy one packet of air, then 5 chips free"*, with its intention to damage the company's reputation. Figure 2 illustrates examples of not-troll memes. The translation of Example 4 would be *"Sorry my friend (girl)"*. As this example does not contain any provoking or offensive content and is even funny, it should be listed in the not-troll category.

As a troll meme is directed towards someone, it is easy to find such content in the comments section or group chat of social media. For our work, we collected memes from volunteers who sent them through WhatsApp, a social media for chatting and creating a group chat. The suspected troll

(a) Example 3

(b) Example 4

Figure 2: Examples of troll and not-troll memes.

memes then have been verified and annotated manually by the annotators. As the users who sent these troll memes belong to the Tamil speaking population, all the troll memes are in Tamil. The general format of the meme is the image and Tamil text embedded within the image.

Most of the troll memes comes from the state of Tamil Nadu, in India. The Tamil language, which has 75 million speakers,[1] belongs to the Dravidian language family (Rao and Lalitha Devi, 2013; Chakravarthi et al., 2019a; Chakravarthi et al., 2019b; Chakravarthi et al., 2019c) and is one of the 22 scheduled languages of India (Dash et al., 2015). As these troll memes can have a negative psychological effect on an individual, a constraint has to be in place for such a conversation. In this work, we are attempting to identify such troll memes by providing a dataset and image classifier to identify these memes.

3. Related Work

Trolling in social media for text has been studied extensively (Bishop, 2013; Bishop, 2014; Mojica de la Vega and Ng, 2018; Malmasi and Zampieri, 2017; Kumar et al., 2018; Kumar, 2019). Opinion manipulation trolling (Mihaylov et al., 2015b; Mihaylov et al., 2015a), troll comments in News Community (Mihaylov and Nakov, 2016), and the role of political trolls (Atanasov et al., 2019) have been studied. All these considered the trolling on text-only media. However, meme consist of images or images with text.

---

[1]https://www.ethnologue.com/language/tam

A related research area is on offensive content detection. Various works in the recent years have investigated Offensive and Aggression content in text (Clarke and Grieve, 2017; Mathur et al., 2018; Nogueira dos Santos et al., 2018; Galery et al., 2018). For images, Gandhi et al. (2019) deals with offensive images and non-compliant logos. They have developed a computer-vision driven offensive and non-compliant image detection algorithm that identifies the offensive content in the image. They have categorized images as offensive if it has nudity, sexually explicit content, abusive text, objects used to promote violence or racially inappropriate content. The classifier takes advantage of a pre-trained object detector to identify the type of object in the image and then sends the image to the unit which specializes in detecting objects in the image. The majority of memes do not contain nudity or explicit sexual content due to the moderation of social media on nudity. Hence unlike their research, we are trying to identify troll memes by using image features derived by use of a convolutional neural network.

Hate speech is a subset of offensive language and datasets associated with hate speech have been collected from social media such as Twitter (Xiang et al., 2012), Instagram (Hosseinmardi et al., 2015), Yahoo (Nobata et al., 2016), YouTube (Dinakar et al., 2012). In all of these works, only text corpora have been used to detect trolling, offensive, aggression and hate speech. Nevertheless, for memes, there is no such dataset. For Indian language memes, it is not available as to our knowledge. We are the first to develop a meme dataset for Tamil, with troll or not-troll annotation.

4. Dataset

4.1. Ethics

For our study, people provided memes voluntarily for our research. Additionally, all personal identifiable information such as usernames are deleted from this dataset. The annotators were warned about the trolling content before viewing the meme, and our instructions informed them that they could quit the annotation campaign anytime if they felt uncomfortable.

4.2. Data collection

To retrieve high-quality meme data that would likely to include trolling, we asked the volunteers to provide us with memes that they get in their social media platforms, like WhatsApp, Facebook, Instagram, and Pinterest. The data was collected between November 1, 2019, until January 15, 2019, from sixteen volunteers. We are not disclosing any personal information of the volunteers such as gender as per their will. Figure 3 shows an example of the collected memes. We removed duplicate memes, however, we kept memes that uses the same image but different text. This was a challenging task since the same meme could have different file names. Hence the same meme could be annotated by different annotators. Due to this, we checked manually and removed such duplicates before sending them to annotators. An example is shown in Figure 3, where the same image with different text is used. Example 5 describes the image as *"can not understand what you are saying"*, whereby Example 6 describes image as *"I am confused"*.

(a) Example 5

(b) Example 6

Figure 3: Examples on same image with different text.

4.3. Annotation

After we obtained the memes, we presented this data to the annotators using Google Forms. To not over-burden the annotators, we provided ten memes per page and hundred memes per form. For each form, the annotators are asked to decide if a given meme is of category troll or not-troll. As a part of annotation guidelines, we gave multiple examples of troll memes and not-troll memes to the annotators. The annotation for these examples has been done by the an annotator who is considered as a expert as well as a native Tamil speaker. Each meme is assigned to two different annotators, a male and a female annotator. To ensure the quality of the annotations and due to the region-specific nature of the annotation task, only native speakers from Tamil Nadu, India were recruited as annotators. Although we are not disclosing the gender demographics of volunteers who provided memes, we have gender-balanced annotation since each meme has been annotated by a male and a female.A meme is considered as troll only when both of the annotators label it as a troll.

4.4. Inter-Annotator Agreement

In order to evaluate the reliability of the annotation and their robustness across experiments, we analyzed the inter-annotator agreement using Cohen's kappa (Cohen, 1960). It compares the probability of two annotators agreeing by chance with the observed agreement. It measures agreement expected by chance by modelling each annotator with separate distribution governing their likelihood of assigning a particular category. Mathematically,

$$K = \frac{p(A) - p(E)}{1 - p(E)} \tag{1}$$

where K is the kappa value, $p(A)$ is the probability of the actual outcome and $p(E)$ is the probability of the expected outcome as predicted by chance (Bloodgood and Grothendieck, 2013). We got a kappa value of 0.62 between two annotators (gender balance male and female annotators). Based on Landis and Koch (1977) and given the inherent obscure nature of memes, we got fair agreement amongst the annotators.

4.5. Data Statistics

We collected 2,969 memes, of which most are images with text embedded on them. After the annotation, we learned that the majority (1,951) of these were annotated as troll memes, and 1,018 as not-troll memes. Furthermore, we observed that memes, which have more than one image have a high probability of being a troll, whereas those with only one image are likely to be not-troll. We included Flickr30K[2] images (Young et al., 2014) to the not-troll category to address the class imbalance. Flickr30K is only added to training, while the test set is randomly chosen from our dataset. In all our experiments the test set remains the same.

5. Methodology

To demonstrate how the given dataset can be used to classify troll memes, we defined two experiments with four variations of each. We measured the performance of the proposed baselines by using precision, recall and F1-score for each class, i.e. "troll and not-troll". We used ResNet (He et al., 2016) and MobileNet (Howard et al., 2017) as a baseline to perform the experiments. We give insights into their architecture and design choices in the sections below.

ResNet

ResNet has won the ImageNet ILSVRC 2015 (Russakovsky et al., 2015) classification task. It is still a popular method for classifying images and uses residual learning which connects low-level and high-level representation directly by skipping the connections in-between. This improves the performance of ResNet by diminishing the problem of vanishing gradient descent. It assumes that a deeper network should not produce higher training error than a shallow network. In this experiment, we used the ResNet architecture with 176 layers. As it was trained on the ImageNet task, we removed the classification (last) layer and used *GlobalAveragePooling* in place of fully connected layer to save the computational cost. Later, we added four fully connected layers with the classification layer which has a sigmoid activation function.This architecture is trained with or without pre-trained ImageNet weights.

MobileNet

We trained MobileNet with and without ImageNet weights. The model has a depth multiplier of 1.4, and an input dimension of 224×224 pixels. This provides a $1,280 \times 1.4 =$

---

[2]https://github.com/BryanPlummer/flickr30k_entities

$1,792$ -dimensional representation of an image, which is then passed through a single hidden layer of a dimensionality of $1,024$ with ReLU activation, before being passed to a hidden layer with input dimension of (512,None) without any activation to provide the final representation h_p. The main purpose of MobileNet is to optimize convolutional neural networks for mobile and embedded vision applications. It is less complex than ResNet in terms of number of hyperparameters and operations. It uses a different convolutional layer for each channel, this allows parallel computation on each channel which is Depthwise Separable Convolution. Later on the features extracted from these layers have been combined using the pointwise convolution layer. We used MobileNet to reduce the computational cost and compare it with the computationally intensive ResNet.

6. Experiments

We experimented with ResNet and MobileNet. The variation in experiments comes in terms of the data on which the models have been trained on, while the test set (300 memes) remained the same for all experiments. In the first variation, *TamilMemes* in Table 1, we trained the ResNet and MobileNet models on our Tamil meme dataset(2,669 memes). The second variation, i.e. *TamilMemes + ImageNet* uses pre-trained ImageNet weights on the Tamil memes dataset. To address the class imbalance, we added 1,000 images from the Flickr30k dataset to the training set in the third variation i.e. *TamilMemes + ImageNet + Flickr1k*. As a result, the third variation has 3,969 images (1,951 trolls and 2,018 not-trolls). In the last variation, *TamilMemes + ImageNet + Flickr30k*, we added 30,000 images from the Flickr30k dataset to not-troll category. Flickr dataset has images and the captions which describes the image. We used these images as a not-troll category because they do not convey trollings without the context of the text. Except for the *TamilMemes* baseline, we are using pre-trained ImageNet weights for all other variations. Images from the Flickr30k dataset are used to balance the not-troll class in the *TamilMemes + ImageNet + Flickr1k* variation. On the one hand, the use of all the samples from the Flickr30k dataset as not-troll in the fourth variation introduces the class imbalance by significantly increasing the number of not-troll samples compared to the troll one. On the other hand, in the first variation, a higher number of troll meme samples again introduces a class imbalance.

7. Result and Discussion

In the ResNet variations, we observed that there is no change in the macro averaged precision, recall and F1-score except for *TamilMemes + ImageNet + Flickr1k* variation. This variation has relatively poor results when compared with the other three variations in ResNet. While precision at identifying the troll class for the ResNet baseline does not vary much, we get better precision at classifying troll memes in the *TamilMemes* variation. This shows that the ResNet model trained on just Tamil memes has a better chance at identifying troll memes. The scenario is different in the case of the MobileNet variations. On the one hand, we observed less precision at identifying the troll class for the TamilMemes variation. On the other

Variations	ResNET							
	TamilMemes				TamilMemes + ImageNet			
	Precision	Recall	f1-score	count	Precision	Recall	f1-score	count
troll	**0.37**	0.33	0.35	100	**0.36**	0.35	0.35	100
not-troll	0.68	0.71	0.70	200	0.68	0.69	0.68	200
macro-avg	**0.52**	**0.52**	**0.52**	300	**0.52**	**0.52**	**0.52**	300
weighted-avg	0.58	0.59	0.58	300	0.57	0.57	0.57	300
Variations	TamilMemes + ImageNet + Flickr1k				TamilMemes + ImageNet + Flickr30k			
troll	**0.30**	0.34	0.32	100	**0.36**	0.35	0.35	100
not-troll	0.64	0.59	0.62	200	0.68	0.69	0.68	200
macro-avg	**0.47**	**0.47**	**0.47**	300	**0.52**	**0.52**	**0.52**	300
weighted-avg	0.53	0.51	0.52	300	0.57	0.57	0.57	300
	MobileNet							
Variations	TamilMemes				TamilMemes + ImageNet			
troll	**0.28**	0.27	0.28	100	**0.34**	0.43	0.38	100
not-troll	0.64	0.66	0.65	200	0.67	0.58	0.62	200
macro-avg	**0.46**	**0.46**	**0.46**	300	**0.50**	**0.51**	**0.50**	300
weighted-avg	0.52	0.53	0.52	300	0.56	0.53	0.54	300
Variations	TamilMemes + ImageNet + Flickr1k				TamilMemes + ImageNet + Flickr30k			
troll	0.33	0.55	0.41	100	0.31	0.34	0.33	100
not-troll	0.66	0.45	0.53	200	0.65	0.62	0.64	200
macro-avg	**0.50**	**0.50**	**0.47**	300	**0.48**	**0.48**	**0.48**	300
weighted-avg	0.55	0.48	0.49	300	0.54	0.53	0.53	300

Table 1: Precision, recall, F1-score and count for ResNet, MobileNet and their variations.

hand, we see improvement in precision at detecting trolls in the TamilMeme + ImageNet variation. This shows that MobileNet can leverage transfer learning to improve results. The relatively poor performance of MobileNet on the TamilMeme variation shows that it can not learn complex features like ResNet does to identify troll memes. For ResNet, the trend in the macro averaged score can be seen increasing in *TamilMemes + ImageNet* and *TamilMemes + ImageNet + Flickr1k* variations when compared to the TamilMemes variation. The *TamilMemes + ImageNet + Flickr30k* variation shows a lower macro averaged score than that of the *TamilMemes + ImageNet + Flickr1k* variation in both MobileNet and ResNet. Overall the precision for troll class identification lies in the range of 0.28 and 0.37, which is rather less than that of the not-troll class which lies in the range of 0.64 and 0.68. When we train ResNet in class imbalanced data in *TamilMemes* and *TamilMemes + ImageNet + Flickr30k* variations, results shows that the macro-averaged score of these variations are not hampered by the class imbalance issue. While for same variations MobileNet shows poor macro-averaged precision and recall score when compared with other variations. This shows that MobileNet is more susceptible to class imbalance issue than ResNet.

8. Conclusions and Future work

As shown in the Table 1 the classification model performs poorly at identifying of troll memes. We observed that this stems from the problem characteristics of memes. The meme dataset is unbalanced and memes have both image and text embedded to it with code-mixing in different forms. Therefore, it is inherently more challenging to train a classifier using just images. Further, the same image can be used with different text to mean different things, potentially making the task more complicated.

To reduce the burden placed on annotators, we plan to use a semi-supervised approach to the size of the dataset. Semi-supervised approaches have been proven to be of good use to increase the size of the datasets for under-resourced scenarios. We plan to use optical character recognizer (OCR) followed by a manual evaluation to obtain the text in the images. Since Tamil memes have code-mixing phenomenon, we plan to tackle the problem accordingly. With text identification using OCR, we will be able to approach the problem in a multi-modal way. We have created a meme dataset only for Tamil, but we plan to extend this to other languages as well.

Acknowledgments

This publication has emanated from research supported in part by a research grant from Science Foundation Ireland (SFI) under Grant Number SFI/12/RC/2289_P2, co-funded by the European Regional Development Fund, as well as by the H2020 project Prêt-à-LLOD under Grant Agreement number 825182.

Bibliographical References

Atanasov, A., De Francisci Morales, G., and Nakov, P. (2019). Predicting the role of political trolls in social media. In *Proceedings of the 23rd Conference on Computational Natural Language Learning (CoNLL)*, pages 1023–1034, Hong Kong, China, November. Association for Computational Linguistics.

Bishop, J. (2013). The effect of de-individuation of the internet troller on criminal procedure implementation: An interview with a hater - proquest. *International journal of cyber criminology*, page 28–48.

Bishop, J. (2014). Dealing with internet trolling in political online communities: Towards the this is why we can't have nice things scale. *Int. J. E-Polit.*, 5(4):1–20, October.

Bloodgood, M. and Grothendieck, J. (2013). Analysis of stopping active learning based on stabilizing predictions. In *Proceedings of the Seventeenth Conference on Computational Natural Language Learning*, pages 10–19, Sofia, Bulgaria, August. Association for Computational Linguistics.

Chakravarthi, B. R., Arcan, M., and McCrae, J. P. (2018). Improving Wordnets for Under-Resourced Languages Using Machine Translation. In *Proceedings of the 9th Global WordNet Conference*. The Global WordNet Conference 2018 Committee.

Chakravarthi, B. R., Arcan, M., and McCrae, J. P. (2019a). Comparison of Different Orthographies for Machine Translation of Under-Resourced Dravidian Languages. In Maria Eskevich, et al., editors, *2nd Conference on Language, Data and Knowledge (LDK 2019)*, volume 70 of *OpenAccess Series in Informatics (OASIcs)*, pages 6:1–6:14, Dagstuhl, Germany. Schloss Dagstuhl–Leibniz-Zentrum fuer Informatik.

Chakravarthi, B. R., Arcan, M., and McCrae, J. P. (2019b). WordNet gloss translation for under-resourced languages using multilingual neural machine translation. In *Proceedings of the Second Workshop on Multilingualism at the Intersection of Knowledge Bases and Machine Translation*, pages 1–7, Dublin, Ireland, August. European Association for Machine Translation.

Chakravarthi, B. R., Priyadharshini, R., Stearns, B., Jayapal, A., S, S., Arcan, M., Zarrouk, M., and McCrae, J. P. (2019c). Multilingual multimodal machine translation for Dravidian languages utilizing phonetic transcription. In *Proceedings of the 2nd Workshop on Technologies for MT of Low Resource Languages*, pages 56–63, Dublin, Ireland, August. European Association for Machine Translation.

Chakravarthi, B. R., Jose, N., Suryawanshi, S., Sherly, E., and McCrae, J. P. (2020a). A sentiment analysis dataset for code-mixed Malayalam-English. In *Proceedings of the 1st Joint Workshop of SLTU (Spoken Language Technologies for Under-resourced languages) and CCURL (Collaboration and Computing for Under-Resourced Languages) (SLTU-CCURL 2020)*, Marseille, France, May. European Language Resources Association (ELRA).

Chakravarthi, B. R., Muralidaran, V., Priyadharshini, R., and McCrae, J. P. (2020b). Corpus creation for sentiment analysis in code-mixed Tamil-English text. In *Proceedings of the 1st Joint Workshop of SLTU (Spoken Language Technologies for Under-resourced languages) and CCURL (Collaboration and Computing for Under-Resourced Languages) (SLTU-CCURL 2020)*, Marseille, France, May. European Language Resources Association (ELRA).

Clarke, I. and Grieve, J. (2017). Dimensions of abusive language on Twitter. In *Proceedings of the First Workshop on Abusive Language Online*, pages 1–10, Vancouver, BC, Canada, August. Association for Computational Linguistics.

Cohen, J. (1960). A Coefficient of Agreement for Nominal Scales. *Educational and Psychological Measurement*, 20(1):37.

Dash, N. S., Selvraj, A., and Hussain, M. (2015). Generating translation corpora in Indic languages:cultivating bilingual texts for cross lingual fertilization. In *Proceedings of the 12th International Conference on Natural Language Processing*, pages 333–342, Trivandrum, India, December. NLP Association of India.

Dinakar, K., Jones, B., Havasi, C., Lieberman, H., and Picard, R. (2012). Common sense reasoning for detection, prevention, and mitigation of cyberbullying. *ACM Trans. Interact. Intell. Syst.*, 2(3), September.

Galery, T., Charitos, E., and Tian, Y. (2018). Aggression identification and multi lingual word embeddings. In *Proceedings of the First Workshop on Trolling, Aggression and Cyberbullying (TRAC-2018)*, pages 74–79, Santa Fe, New Mexico, USA, August. Association for Computational Linguistics.

Gandhi, S., Kokkula, S., Chaudhuri, A., Magnani, A., Stanley, T., Ahmadi, B., Kandaswamy, V., Ovenc, O., and Mannor, S. (2019). Image matters: Detecting offensive and non-compliant content/logo in product images. *arXiv preprint arXiv:1905.02234*.

He, K., Zhang, X., Ren, S., and Sun, J. (2016). Deep residual learning for image recognition. In *2016 IEEE Conference on Computer Vision and Pattern Recognition, CVPR 2016, Las Vegas, NV, USA, June 27-30, 2016*, pages 770–778.

Hosseinmardi, H., Mattson, S. A., Rafiq, R. I., Han, R., Lv, Q., and Mishra, S. (2015). Analyzing labeled cyberbullying incidents on the instagram social network. In *International conference on social informatics*, pages 49–66. Springer.

Howard, A. G., Zhu, M., Chen, B., Kalenichenko, D., Wang, W., Weyand, T., Andreetto, M., and Adam, H. (2017). Mobilenets: Efficient convolutional neural networks for mobile vision applications. *arXiv preprint arXiv:1704.04861*.

Jose, N., Chakravarthi, B. R., Suryawanshi, S., Sherly, E., and McCrae, J. P. (2020). A survey of current datasets for code-switching research. In *2020 6th International Conference on Advanced Computing and Communication Systems (ICACCS)*.

Kumar, R., Ojha, A. K., Malmasi, S., and Zampieri, M. (2018). Benchmarking aggression identification in social media. In *Proceedings of the First Workshop on Trolling, Aggression and Cyberbullying (TRAC-2018)*, pages 1–11, Santa Fe, New Mexico, USA, August. Association for Computational Linguistics.

Kumar, R. (2019). # shutdownjnu vs# standwithjnu: A study of aggression and conflict in political debates on social media in india. *Journal of Language Aggression and Conflict*.

Landis, J. R. and Koch, G. G. (1977). The measurement of observer agreement for categorical data. *Biometrics*,

33(1):159–174.

Malmasi, S. and Zampieri, M. (2017). Detecting hate speech in social media. In *Proceedings of the International Conference Recent Advances in Natural Language Processing, RANLP 2017*, pages 467–472, Varna, Bulgaria, September. INCOMA Ltd.

Mathur, P., Shah, R., Sawhney, R., and Mahata, D. (2018). Detecting offensive tweets in Hindi-English code-switched language. In *Proceedings of the Sixth International Workshop on Natural Language Processing for Social Media*, pages 18–26, Melbourne, Australia, July. Association for Computational Linguistics.

Mihaylov, T. and Nakov, P. (2016). Hunting for troll comments in news community forums. In *Proceedings of the 54th Annual Meeting of the Association for Computational Linguistics (Volume 2: Short Papers)*, pages 399–405, Berlin, Germany, August. Association for Computational Linguistics.

Mihaylov, T., Georgiev, G., and Nakov, P. (2015a). Finding opinion manipulation trolls in news community forums. In *Proceedings of the Nineteenth Conference on Computational Natural Language Learning*, pages 310–314, Beijing, China, July. Association for Computational Linguistics.

Mihaylov, T., Koychev, I., Georgiev, G., and Nakov, P. (2015b). Exposing paid opinion manipulation trolls. In *Proceedings of the International Conference Recent Advances in Natural Language Processing*, pages 443–450, Hissar, Bulgaria, September. INCOMA Ltd. Shoumen, BULGARIA.

Mojica de la Vega, L. G. and Ng, V. (2018). Modeling trolling in social media conversations. In *Proceedings of the Eleventh International Conference on Language Resources and Evaluation (LREC 2018)*, Miyazaki, Japan, May. European Language Resources Association (ELRA).

Nobata, C., Tetreault, J., Thomas, A., Mehdad, Y., and Chang, Y. (2016). Abusive language detection in online user content. In *Proceedings of the 25th international conference on world wide web*, pages 145–153.

Nogueira dos Santos, C., Melnyk, I., and Padhi, I. (2018). Fighting offensive language on social media with unsupervised text style transfer. In *Proceedings of the 56th Annual Meeting of the Association for Computational Linguistics (Volume 2: Short Papers)*, pages 189–194, Melbourne, Australia, July. Association for Computational Linguistics.

Priyadharshini, R., Chakravarthi, B. R., Vegupatti, M., and McCrae, J. P. (2020). Named entity recognition for code-mixed Indian corpus using meta embedding. In *2020 6th International Conference on Advanced Computing and Communication Systems (ICACCS)*.

Rani, P., Suryawanshi, S., Goswami, K., Chakravarthi, B. R., Fransen, T., and McCrae, J. P. (2020). A comparative study of different state-of-the-art hate speech detection methods for Hindi-English code-mixed data. In *Proceedings of the Second Workshop on Trolling, Aggression and Cyberbullying*, Marseille, France, May. European Language Resources Association (ELRA).

Ranjan, P., Raja, B., Priyadharshini, R., and Balabantaray, R. C. (2016). A comparative study on code-mixed data of Indian social media vs formal text. In *2016 2nd International Conference on Contemporary Computing and Informatics (IC3I)*, pages 608–611, Dec.

Rao, T. P. R. K. and Lalitha Devi, S. (2013). Tamil English cross lingual information retrieval. In Prasenjit Majumder, et al., editors, *Multilingual Information Access in South Asian Languages*, pages 269–279, Berlin, Heidelberg. Springer Berlin Heidelberg.

Russakovsky, O., Deng, J., Su, H., Krause, J., Satheesh, S., Ma, S., Huang, Z., Karpathy, A., Khosla, A., Bernstein, M., Berg, A. C., and Fei-Fei, L. (2015). ImageNet Large Scale Visual Recognition Challenge. *International Journal of Computer Vision (IJCV)*, 115(3):211–252.

Suryawanshi, S., Chakravarthi, B. R., Arcan, M., and Buitelaar, P. (2020). Multimodal meme dataset (MultiOFF) for identifying offensive content in image and text. In *Proceedings of the Second Workshop on Trolling, Aggression and Cyberbullying*, Marseille, France, May. European Language Resources Association (ELRA).

Wang, W. Y. and Wen, M. (2015). I can has cheezburger? a nonparanormal approach to combining textual and visual information for predicting and generating popular meme descriptions. In *Proceedings of the 2015 Conference of the North American Chapter of the Association for Computational Linguistics: Human Language Technologies*, pages 355–365, Denver, Colorado, May–June. Association for Computational Linguistics.

Xiang, G., Fan, B., Wang, L., Hong, J., and Rose, C. (2012). Detecting offensive tweets via topical feature discovery over a large scale twitter corpus. In *Proceedings of the 21st ACM international conference on Information and knowledge management*, pages 1980–1984.

Young, P., Lai, A., Hodosh, M., and Hockenmaier, J. (2014). From image descriptions to visual denotations: New similarity metrics for semantic inference over event descriptions. *TACL*, 2:67–78.

Proceedings of the WILDRE5– 5th Workshop on Indian Language Data: Resources and Evaluation, pages 14–19
Language Resources and Evaluation Conference (LREC 2020), Marseille, 11–16 May 2020
© European Language Resources Association (ELRA), licensed under CC-BY-NC

OdiEnCorp 2.0: Odia-English Parallel Corpus for Machine Translation

Shantipriya Parida[1]   **Satya Ranjan Dash**[2]   **Ondřej Bojar**[3*]
Petr Motlíček[1]   **Priyanka Pattnaik**[2]   **Debasish Kumar Mallick**[2]
[1]Idiap Research Institute, Martigny, Switzerland
{shantipriya.parida, petr.motlicek}@idiap.ch
[2]KIIT University, Bhubaneswar, India
sdashfca@kiit.ac.in, priyankapattanaik2013@gmail.com,
mdebasishkumar@gmail.com
[3]Charles University, Prague, Czech Republic
bojar@ufal.mff.cuni.cz

Abstract

The preparation of parallel corpora is a challenging task, particularly for languages that suffer from under-representation in the digital world. In a multi-lingual country like India, the need for such parallel corpora is stringent for several low-resource languages. In this work, we provide an extended English-Odia parallel corpus, OdiEnCorp 2.0, aiming particularly at Neural Machine Translation (NMT) systems which will help translate English↔Odia. OdiEnCorp 2.0 includes existing English-Odia corpora and we extended the collection by several other methods of data acquisition: parallel data scraping from many websites, including Odia Wikipedia, but also optical character recognition (OCR) to extract parallel data from scanned images. Our OCR-based data extraction approach for building a parallel corpus is suitable for other low resource languages that lack in online content. The resulting OdiEnCorp 2.0 contains 98,302 sentences and 1.69 million English and 1.47 million Odia tokens. To the best of our knowledge, OdiEnCorp 2.0 is the largest Odia-English parallel corpus covering different domains and available freely for non-commercial and research purposes.

Keywords: Parallel Corpus, Machine Translation (MT), Optical Character Recognition (OCR)

1. Introduction

Odia (also called Oriya) is an Indian language belonging to the Indo-Aryan branch of the Indo-European language family. It is the predominant language of the Indian state of Odisha. Odia is one of the 22 official languages and 14 regional languages of India. Odia is the sixth Indian language to be designated a Classical Language in India based on having a long literary history and not having borrowed extensively from other languages.[1] Odia is written in Odia script, which is a Brahmic script. Odia has its origins pinned to the 10th century. In the 16th and 17th centuries, as in the case of other Indian languages, Odia too suffered changes due to the influence of Sanskrit.[2] Odia is nowadays spoken by 50 million speakers.[3] It is heavily influenced by the Dravidian languages as well as Arabic, Persian, English. Odias inflectional morphology is rich with a three-tier tense system. The prototypical word order is subject-object-verb (SOV).

In today's digital world, there has been a demand for machine translation systems for English↔Odia translation for a long time which couldn't have been fulfilled due to the lack of Odia resources, particularly a parallel corpus. Parallel corpora are of great importance in language studies, teaching and many natural language processing applications such as machine translation, cross-language information retrieval, word sense disambiguation, bilingual terminology extraction as well as induction of tools across languages. The Odia language is not available in many machine translation systems. Several researchers explored these goals, developing Odia resources and prototype machine translation systems but these are not available online and benefitting users (Das et al., 2018; Balabantaray and Sahoo, 2013; Rautaray et al., 2019).

We have analysed the available English-Odia parallel corpora (OdiEnCorp 1.0, PMIndia) and their performance (BLEU score) for machine translation (Parida et al., 2020; Haddow and Kirefu, 2020). OdiEnCorp 1.0 contains Odia-English parallel and monolingual data. The statistics of OdiEnCorp 1.0 are shown in Table 1. In OdiEnCorp 1.0, the parallel sentences are mostly derived from the English-Odia parallel Bible and the size of the parallel corpus (29K) is not sufficient for neural machine translation (NMT) as documented by the baseline results (Parida et al., 2020) as well as attempts at improving them using NMT techniques such as transfer learning (Kocmi and Bojar, 2019).

The recently released PMIndia corpus (Haddow and Kirefu, 2020) contains 38K English-Odia parallel sentences but it is mostly collected from the prime minister of India's official portal[4] containing text about government policies in 13 official languages of India.

These points motivate us for building OdiEnCorp 2.0 with more data, covering various domains suitable for various tasks of language processing, but particularly for the building of an English↔Odia machine translation system which will be useful for the research community as well as general users for non-commercial purposes.

---

* Corresponding author

[1]https://infogalactic.com/info/Odia_language

[2]https://www.indianmirror.com/languages/odiya-language.html

[3]https://www.britannica.com/topic/Oriya-language

[4]https://www.pmindia.gov.in/en/

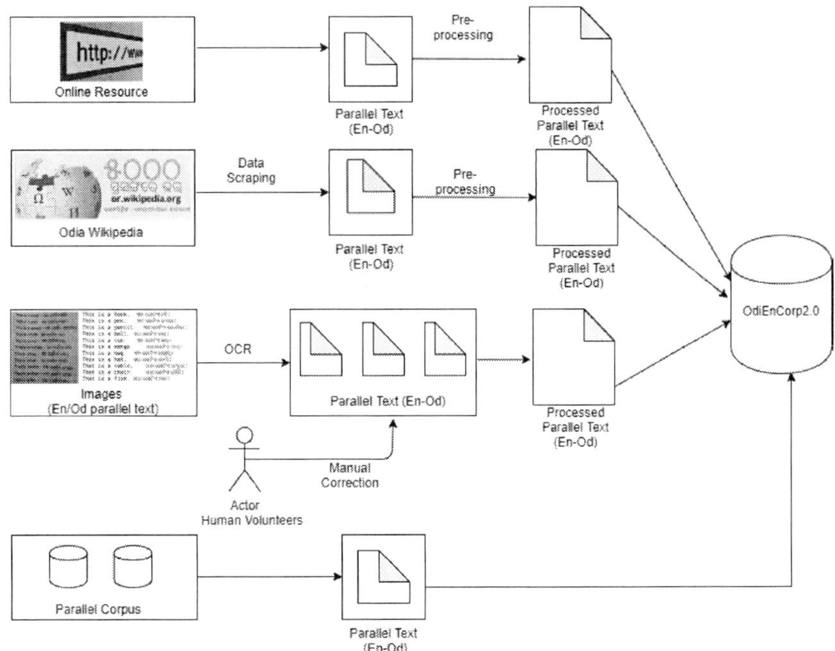

Figure 1: Block diagram of the Corpus building process. The parallel data collected from various sources (online/offline) and processed using both automatic and manual processing to build the final Corpus OdiEnCorp 2.0.

Source	Sentences	Tokens	
	(Parallel)	English	Odia
English-Odia Parallel Bible	29069	756861	640157
Odisha Government Portal	122	1044	930
Odisha Govt Home Department Portal	82	367	327
Odia Digital Library (Odia Bibhaba)	393	7524	6233
Odia Digital Library (Odia Virtual Academy)	31	453	378
Total	29697	766249	648025

Table 1: Statistics of OdiEnCorp 1.0.

2. Data Sources

As there is a very limited number of online Odia resources available, we have explored several possible ways to collect Odia-English parallel data. Although these methods need a considerable amount of manual processing, we opted for them, to achieve the largest possible data size. In sum, we used these sources:

- Data extracted using OCR,

- Data extracted from Odia Wikipedia,

- Data extracted from other online resources,

- Data reused from existing corpora.

The overall process of the OdiEnCorp 2.0 is shown in Figure 1.

2.1. OCR-Based Text Extraction

Many books are translated in more than one language and they could serve as a reliable source to obtain parallel sentences, but they are unfortunately not digitized (Bakliwal et al., 2016; Premjith et al., 2016). OCR technology has improved substantially, which has allowed for large-scale digitization of textual resources such as books, old newspapers, ancient hand-written documents (Dhondt et al., 2017). That said, it should be kept in mind that there are often mistakes in the scanned texts as OCR system occasionally misrecognizes letters or falsely identifies text regions, leading to misspellings and linguistics errors in the output text (Afli et al., 2016).

Odia language has a rich literary heritage and many books are available in printed form. We have explored books having either English and Odia parallel text together or books having both versions (English and Odia). We have used the study, translation, grammar, literature, and motivational books for this purpose, obtaining the source images either from the web, or directly scanning them ourselves.

We start with the image containing the Odia language text represented in the RGB color space. For the Odia text recognition, we use the "Tesseract OCR engine" (Smith, 2007) with several improvements in the pre-processing phase.

First, we move from the traditional method which converts RGB to grayscale by taking the simple average of the three channels. We convert the RGB image into a grayscale image

This is a book.	ଏହା ଗୋଟିଏ ବହି ।
This is a pen.	ଏହା ଗୋଟିଏ କଲମ ।
This is a pencil.	ଏହା ଗୋଟିଏ ପେନ୍‌ସିଲ ।
This is a ball.	ଏହା ଗୋଟିଏ ବଲ୍ ।
This is a cup.	ଏହା ଗୋଟିଏ କପ୍ ।
This is a mango.	ଏହା ଗୋଟିଏ ଆମ୍ବ ।
This is a bag.	ଏହା ଗୋଟିଏ ବ୍ୟାଗ୍ ।
This is a hat.	ଏହା ଗୋଟିଏ ଟୋପି ।
That is a table.	ତାହା ଗୋଟିଏ ଟେବୁଲ୍ ।
That is a chair.	ତାହା ଗୋଟିଏ ଚୌକି ।
That is a fish.	ତାହା ଗୋଟିଏ ମାଛ ।

(a) Sample scanned image of parallel (English-Odia) data.

(b) Extracted parallel data.

Figure 2: An illustration of the scanned image containing parallel English-Odia data and extracted data.

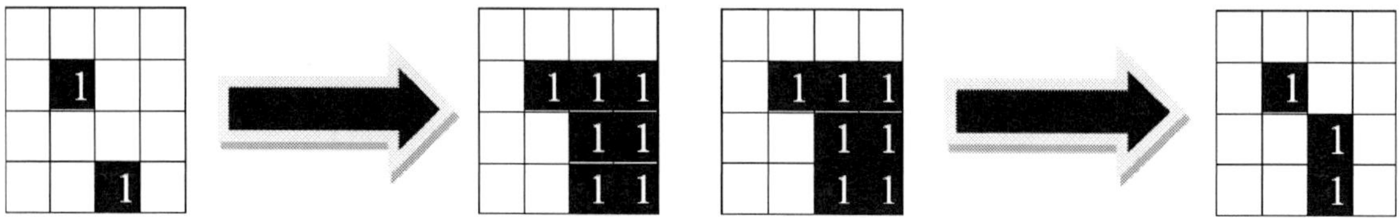

Figure 3: Dilation

Figure 4: Erosion

by applying the luminosity method which also averages the values, but it takes a weighted average to account for human perception (Joshi, 2019):

$$\text{Grayscale} = 0.299R + 0.587G + 0.114B \qquad (1)$$

where R is the amount of red, G green and B blue color in a pixel.

To change the image further to black and white only, "Tesseract" uses the traditional binarization algorithm called "Otsu". We use instead the "Niblack and Sauvola threshold algorithm" which we found to give better results. The advantage of the Niblack algorithm is that it slides a rectangular window through the image (Smith, 2007). The center pixel threshold T is derived from the mean m and variance s values inside the window.

$$T = m + k \cdot s, \qquad (2)$$

where k is a constant set to 0.8.

"Niblack" can create noise in some areas of the image, so we further improve it by including the "Sauvola" algorithm. Thus the modified formula is:

$$T = m \cdot \left(1 - k \cdot \left(1 - \frac{s}{R}\right)\right), \qquad (3)$$

where R is the dynamics of standard deviation, a constant set to 128.

This formula will not detect all the images of documents. So the normalized formula we have implemented is:

$$T = m - k \cdot \left(1 - \frac{s}{R}\right) \cdot (m - M), \qquad (4)$$

where R is the maximum standard deviation of all the windows and M is the gray level of the current image.

However, some black pixels vanish during these processes which may lead to erroneous character recognition, so we use Dilation (Gaikwad and Mahender, 2016) to join areas which got accidentally disconnected, see Figure 3 for an illustration.

Because dilation sometimes produces too many black pixels, we further apply "Erosion" (Alginahi, 2010) as illustrated in Figure 4.

Finally, Figure 2 illustrates a sample of the scanned image containing parallel Odia-English data and the extracted text.

2.2. Odia Wikipedia

The Odia Wikipedia started in 2002 and serves as a good source for Odia-English parallel data. The following steps were performed to obtain parallel sentences from Odia Wikipedia, with more details provided in the sections below:

1. Collect Wikipedia dump (20th October 2019) for the language pair Odia-English.

2. Clean the text by removing references, URLs, instructions, or any unnecessary contents.

3. Segment articles into sentences, relying on English/Odia full stop mark.

4. Align sentences between Odia and English.

Source	Sentences	Tokens		Book Name and Author
		English	Odia	(Parallel)
Wikipedia Dump	5796	38249	37944	-
Glosbe Website	6222	40143	38248	-
Odisha District Website	761	15227	13132	-
TamilCube Website	4434	7180	6776	-
OCR (Book 1)	356	4825	3909	A Tiger at Twilight by Manoj Dash
OCR (Book 2)	9499	117454	102279	Yajnaseni by Prativa Ray
OCR (Book 3)	775	13936	12068	Wings of Fire by APJ Abdul Kalam with Arun Tiwari
OCR (Book 4)	1211	1688	1652	Word Book by Shibashis Kar and Shreenath Chaterjee
OCR (Book 5)	293	1492	1471	Spoken English by Partha Sarathi Panda and Prakhita Padhi
Odia Virtual Academy (OVA)	1021	4297	3653	Sarala (Tribhasi) Bhasa Sikhana Petika
PMIndia	38588	690634	607611	-
OdiEnCorp 1.0	29346	756967	648025	-
Total	98302	1692092	1476768	

Table 2: OdiEnCorp 2.0 parallel corpus details. Training, dev and test sets together.

2.3. Additional Online Resources

Finding potential parallel texts in a collection of web documents is a challenging task, see e.g. (Antonova and Misyurev, 2011; Kúdela et al., 2017; Schwenk, 2018; Artetxe and Schwenk, 2019).

We have explored websites and prepared a list of such websites which are potential for us to collect Odia-English parallel data. The websites were then crawled with a simple Python script.

We found Odisha's government portals of each district (e.g. Nayagarh district[5]) of Odisha containing general information about the district in both English and Odia version. Analyzing extracted text, we found a few cases where English was repeated in both sides of the website. We have aligned the extracted text manually to obtain the parallel text.

We also extracted parallel data from the Odia digital library "Odia Virtual Academy",[6] an Odisha government-initiated portal to store treasures of Odia language and literature for seamless access to Odia people staying across the globe. The web page provides tri-lingual books (tribal dictionary[7] containing common words and their translations in English and Odia) and we extracted the English-Odia sentence pairs from it.

2.4. Reusing Available Corpora

Finally, we included parallel data from OdiEnCorp 1.0 and PMIndia (Parida et al., 2020; Haddow and Kirefu, 2020). Both corpora contain pre-processed English-Odia parallel sentences. The statistics of these corpora are available in Table 2.

3. Data Processing

The data collected from different sources were processed to achieve a unified format.

3.1. Extraction of Plain Text

When utilizing online resources, we used a Python script to scrape plain text from HTML pages.

[5] https://nayagarh.nic.in
[6] https://ova.gov.in/en/
[7] https://ova.gov.in/de/
odisha-tribal-dictionary-and-language/

3.2. Manual Processing

After analyzing the raw data extracted using the OCR-based approach, we found a few errors such as unnecessary characters and symbols, missing words, etc. One of the reasons of poor OCR performance was the fact that some images were taken using mobile phones. In later processing, we always used a proper scanner.

We decided for manual correction of such entries by volunteers whose mother tongue is Odia. Although this task is time-consuming and tedious, the result should be of considerably better quality and much more suitable for machine translation and other NLP tasks.

Four volunteers worked part-time (2-3 hours daily) for four months on scanning of books, extracting data from the scanned images using OCR techniques, collecting data from online as well as offline sources, and post-editing all the data collected from different sources.

3.3. Sentence Segmentation

All sources that come in paragraphs (e.g. Wikipedia articles or books) had to be segmented into sentences. We considered full stop (.) as of the end of the sentence for English and Odia Danda or Purnaviram (|) as of the end of the sentence for Odia language.

3.4. Sentence Alignment

For some sources, the alignment between English and Odia sentences was straightforward. Sources like Odia Wikipedia posed a bigger challenge, because the texts in the two languages are often created or edited independently of each other.

To achieve the best possible parallel corpus, we relied on manual sentence alignment. In this process, we had to truncate or remove several few sentences in either of the languages in order to reach exactly 1-1 aligned English-Odia sentence pairs.

3.5. Domain Coverage

The resulting corpus OdiEnCorp 2.0 covers a wide variety of domains, esp. compared to similar corpora. Our corpus covers the bible, literature, government policies, daily usage, learning, general domain (Wikipedia).

Dataset	#Sentences	#Tokens EN	#Tokens OD
Train 2.0	69260	1340371	1164636
Dev 2.0	13429	157951	140384
Test 2.0	14163	185957	164532

Table 3: OdiEnCorp 2.0 *processed for NMT experiments.*

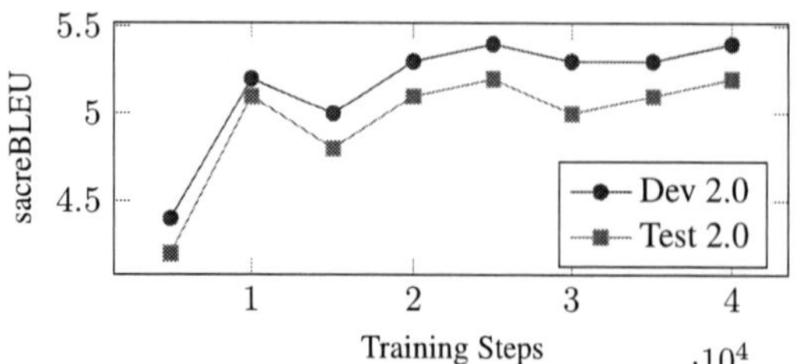

Figure 5: Learning curve (EN→OD)

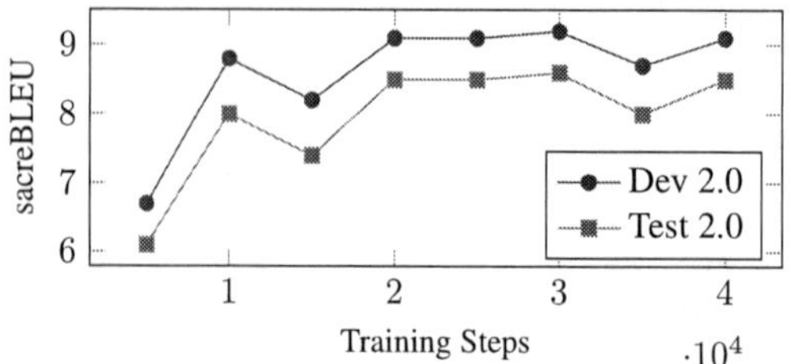

Figure 6: Learning curve (OD→EN)

Training Corpus	Task	sacreBLEU Dev 2.0	sacreBLEU Test 2.0
OdiEnCorp 2.0	EN-OD	5.4	5.2
OdiEnCorp 2.0	OD-EN	9.2	8.6

Table 4: Results for baseline NMT on Dev and Test sets for OdiEnCorp 2.0.

4. Final Data Sizes

The composition of OdiEnCorp 2.0 with statistics for individual sources is provided in Table 2.

The release designates which parts of the corpus should be used for training, which for development and which for final testing. This division of OdiEnCorp 2.0 respects the dev and test sets of OdiEnCorp 1.0, so that models trained on v.2.0 training set can be directly tested on the older v.1.0 dev and test sets.

5. Baseline Neural Machine Translation

For future reference, we provide a very baseline experiment with neural machine translation using OdiEnCorp 2.0 data.

5.1. Dataset Description

For the purpose of NMT training, we removed duplicated sentence pairs and shuffled the segments The training, dev and test set sizes after this processing are shown in Table 3.

5.2. Neural Machine Translation Setup

We used the Transformer model (Vaswani et al., 2018) as implemented in OpenNMT-py (Klein et al., 2017).[8] Subword units were constructed using the word pieces algorithm (Johnson et al., 2017). Tokenization is handled automatically as part of the pre-processing pipeline of word pieces.

We generated the vocabulary of 32k sub-word types jointly for both the source and target languages, sharing it between the encoder and decoder. To train the model, we used a single GPU and followed the standard "Noam" learning rate decay,[9] see (Vaswani et al., 2017) or (Popel and Bojar, 2018) for more details. Our starting learning rate was 0.2 and we used 8000 warm-up steps. The learning curves are shown in Figure 5 and Figure 6,

5.3. Results

We use sacreBLEU[10,11] for estimating translation quality. Based on the Dev 2.0 best score, we select the model at iteration 40k for EN→OD and at 30k for OD→EN to obtain the final test set scores.

Table 4 reports the performance on the Dev and Test sets of OdiEnCorp 2.0. Table 5 uses the Dev and Test sets belonging to OdiEnCorp 1.0. The results in Table 5 thus allow us to observe the gains compared to the scores reported in Parida et al. (2020).

6. Availability

OdiEnCorp 2.0 is available for research and non-commercial use under a Creative Commons Attribution-NonCommercial-ShareAlike 4.0 License, CC-BY-NC-SA[12] at:

http://hdl.handle.net/11234/1-3211

7. Conclusion and Future Work

We presented OdiEnCorp 2.0, an updated version of Odia-English parallel corpus aimed for linguistic research and applications in natural language processing, primarily machine translation.

The corpus will be used for low resource machine translation shared tasks. The first such task is WAT 2020[13] Indic shared task on Odia↔English machine translation.

Our plans for future include:

- Extending OdiEnCorp 2.0 with more parallel data, again by finding various new sources.

- Building an English↔Odia translation system utilizing the developed OdiEnCorp 2.0 corpus and other techniques (back translation, domain adaptation) and releasing it to users for non-commercial purposes.

---

[8] http://opennmt.net/OpenNMT-py/quickstart.html

[9] https://nvidia.github.io/OpenSeq2Seq/html/api-docs/optimizers.html

[10] https://github.com/mjpost/sacreBLEU

[11] Signature: BLEU+c.mixed+#.1+s.exp+tok.13a+v.1.4.3

[12] https://creativecommons.org/licenses/by-nc-sa/4.0/

[13] https://lotus.kuee.kyoto-u.ac.jp/WAT/WAT2020/index.html

		sacreBLEU	
Training Corpus	Task	Dev 1.0	Test 1.0
OdiEnCorp 1.0	EN-OD	4.3	4.1
OdiEnCorp 2.0	EN-OD	4.9	4.0
OdiEnCorp 1.0	OD-EN	9.4	8.6
OdiEnCorp 2.0	OD-EN	12.0	9.3

Table 5: Scores on Dev and Test sets of OdiEnCorp 1.0 for the baseline NMT models trained on OdiEnCorp 1.0 vs. OdiEnCorp 2.0.

- Promoting the corpus in other reputed machine translation campaigns focusing on low resource languages.

8. Acknowledgements

The work was supported by an innovation project (under an Inno-Suisse grant) oriented to improve the automatic speech recognition and natural language understanding technologies for German (Title: SM2: Extracting Semantic Meaning from Spoken Material funding application no. 29814.1 IP-ICT). In part, it was also supported by the EU H2020 project "Real-time network, text, and speaker analytics for combating organized crime" (ROXANNE, grant agreement: 833635) and by the grant 18-24210S of the Czech Science Foundation.

This work has been using language resources and tools stored and distributed by the LINDAT/CLARIN project of the Ministry of Education, Youth and Sports of the Czech Republic (projects LM2015071 and OP VVV VI CZ.02.1.01/0.0/0.0/16 013/0001781).

Afli, H., Barrault, L., and Schwenk, H. (2016). Ocr error correction using statistical machine translation. *Int. J. Comput. Linguistics Appl.*, 7(1):175–191.

Alginahi, Y. (2010). Preprocessing techniques in character recognition. *Character recognition*, 1:1–19.

Antonova, A. and Misyurev, A. (2011). Building a web-based parallel corpus and filtering out machine-translated text. In *Proceedings of the 4th Workshop on Building and Using Comparable Corpora: Comparable Corpora and the Web*, pages 136–144. Association for Computational Linguistics.

Artetxe, M. and Schwenk, H. (2019). Massively multilingual sentence embeddings for zero-shot cross-lingual transfer and beyond. *Transactions of the Association for Computational Linguistics*, 7:597610, Mar.

Bakliwal, P., Devadath, V., and Jawahar, C. (2016). Align me: A framework to generate parallel corpus using ocrs and bilingual dictionaries. In *Proc. of the 6th Workshop on South and Southeast Asian Natural Language Processing (WSSANLP2016)*, pages 183–187.

Balabantaray, R. and Sahoo, D. (2013). An experiment to create parallel corpora for odia. *International Journal of Computer Applications*, 67(19).

Das, A. K., Pradhan, M., Dash, A. K., Pradhan, C., and Das, H. (2018). A constructive machine translation system for english to odia translation. In *2018 International Conference on Communication and Signal Processing (ICCSP)*, pages 0854–0857. IEEE.

Dhondt, E., Grouin, C., and Grau, B. (2017). Generating a training corpus for ocr post-correction using encoder-decoder model. In *Proc. of IJCNLP (Volume 1: Long Papers)*, pages 1006–1014.

Gaikwad, D. K. and Mahender, C. N. (2016). A review paper on text summarization. *International Journal of Advanced Research in Computer and Communication Engineering*, 5(3):154–160.

Haddow, B. and Kirefu, F. (2020). Pmindia–a collection of parallel corpora of languages of india. *arXiv preprint arXiv:2001.09907*.

Johnson, M., Schuster, M., Le, Q. V., Krikun, M., Wu, Y., Chen, Z., Thorat, N., Viégas, F., Wattenberg, M., Corrado, G., Hughes, M., and Dean, J. (2017). Google's multilingual neural machine translation system: Enabling zero-shot translation. *Transactions of the Association for Computational Linguistics*, 5:339–351.

Joshi, N. (2019). Text image extraction and summarization. *Asian Journal For Convergence In Technology (AJCT)*.

Klein, G., Kim, Y., Deng, Y., Senellart, J., and Rush, A. M. (2017). OpenNMT: Open-source toolkit for neural machine translation. In *Proc. ACL*.

Kocmi, T. and Bojar, O. (2019). Transfer learning across languages from someone else's NMT model. *arXiv preprint arXiv:1909.10955*.

Kúdela, J., Holubová, I., and Bojar, O. (2017). Extracting parallel paragraphs from common crawl. *The Prague Bulletin of Mathematical Linguistics*, (107):36–59.

Parida, S., Bojar, O., and Dash, S. R. (2020). OdiEnCorp: Odia–English and Odia-Only Corpus for Machine Translation. In *Smart Intelligent Computing and Applications*, pages 495–504. Springer.

Popel, M. and Bojar, O. (2018). Training tips for the transformer model. *The Prague Bulletin of Mathematical Linguistics*, 110(1):43–70.

Premjith, B., Kumar, S. S., Shyam, R., Kumar, M. A., and Soman, K. (2016). A fast and efficient framework for creating parallel corpus. *Indian J. Sci. Technol*, 9:1–7.

Rautaray, J., Hota, A., and Gochhayat, S. S. (2019). A shallow parser-based hindi to odia machine translation system. In *Computational Intelligence in Data Mining*, pages 51–62. Springer.

Schwenk, H. (2018). Filtering and mining parallel data in a joint multilingual space. In *Proc. of ACL (Volume 2: Short Papers)*, pages 228–234. Association for Computational Linguistics, July.

Smith, R. (2007). An overview of the tesseract ocr engine. In *Ninth International Conference on Document Analysis and Recognition (ICDAR 2007)*, volume 2, pages 629–633. IEEE.

Vaswani, A., Shazeer, N., Parmar, N., Uszkoreit, J., Jones, L., Gomez, A. N., Kaiser, Ł., and Polosukhin, I. (2017). Attention is all you need. In *Advances in Neural Information Processing Systems*, pages 5998–6008.

Vaswani, A., Bengio, S., Brevdo, E., Chollet, F., Gomez, A., Gouws, S., Jones, L., Kaiser, Ł., Kalchbrenner, N., Parmar, N., Sepassi, R., Shazeer, N., and Uszkoreit, J. (2018). Tensor2tensor for neural machine translation. In *Proc. of AMTA (Volume 1: Research Papers)*, pages 193–199.

Handling Noun-Noun Coreference in Tamil

Vijay Sundar Ram and Sobha Lalitha Devi
AU-KBC Research Centre
MIT Campus of Anna University
Chromepet, Chennai, India
sobha@au-kbc.org

Abstract
Natural language understanding by automatic tools is the vital requirement for document processing tools. To achieve it, automatic system has to understand the coherence in the text. Co-reference chains bring coherence to the text. The commonly occurring reference markers which bring cohesiveness are Pronominal, Reflexives, Reciprocals, Distributives, One-anaphors, Noun–noun reference. Here in this paper, we deal with noun-noun reference in Tamil. We present the methodology to resolve these noun-noun anaphors and also present the challenges in handling the noun-noun anaphoric relations in Tamil.

Keywords: Tamil, noun-noun anaphors, Error analysis

1. Introduction

The major challenge in automatic processing of text is making the computer understand the cohesiveness of the text. Cohesion in text is brought by various phenomena in languages namely, Reference, Substitution, Ellipsis, Conjunction and Lexical cohesion (Halliday & Hasan 1976). The commonly occurring reference markers which bring cohesiveness are Pronominal, Reflexives, Reciprocals, Distributives, One-anaphors, Noun–noun reference. The coreference chains are formed using them. Coreference chains are formed by grouping various anaphoric expressions referring to the same entity. These coreference chains are vital in understanding the text. It is required in building sophisticated Natural Language Understanding (NLU) applications. In the present work, we focus on resolution of noun-noun anaphors, which is one of the most frequently occurring reference entities. A noun phrase can be referred by a shorten noun phrases or an acronym, alias or by a synonym words. We describe our machine learning technique based approach on noun-noun anaphora resolution in Tamil text and discussed the challenges in the handling the different types of noun-noun anaphora relations. We have explained noun-noun anaphora relation with the example below.

Ex 1. a
taktar apthul kalam   *oru*   *vinvezi*
Dr(N) Abdul(N) Kalam(N) one(QC) aerospace(N)

vinnaani.
scientist(N).
(Dr. Abdul Kalam was an aerospace scientist.)

Ex 1. b
kalam   *em.i.ti-yil*   *padiththavar.*
Kalam(N) M.I.T(N)+loc study(V)+past+3sh
(Kalam studied in MIT.)

Consider the discourse in Ex.1, 'taktar apthul kalam' (Dr. Abdul Kalam) in sentence Ex.1.a is mentioned as 'kalaam' (Kalam) in Ex.1.b.

One of the early works was by Soon et. al. (2001) where they have used Decision tree, a machine learning based approach for co-reference resolution. They have performed as pair-wise approach using Distance, String Match, Definite Noun phrase, Demonstrative noun phrase, both proper nouns, Appositives as features in the machine

learning technique to resolve the noun-noun anaphors. Ng & Cardie (2002) extended Soon et. al. (2001) work by including lexical, grammatical, semantic, and PoS features. Culcotta et al. (2007) has performed first order probabilistic model for generating co-reference chain, where they have used WordNet, substring match as features to resolve the noun-noun relation. Bengston & Roth (2008) has presented an analysis using refined feature set for pair-wise classification. Rahman & Ng (2009) has proposed a cluster-ranking based approach. Raghunathan et. al (2010) has used multiple sieve based approach. Niton et al (2018) has used a deep neural network based approach. In the following section we have presented in the characteristics of Tamil, which make Noun-Noun anaphora resolution in Tamil a challenging task.

2. Characteristics of Tamil

Tamil belongs to the South Dravidian family of languages. It is a verb final language and allows scrambling. It has post-positions, the genitive precedes the head noun in the genitive phrase and the complementizer follows the embedded clause. Adjective, participial adjectives and free relatives precede the head noun. It is a nominative-accusative language like the other Dravidian languages. The subject of a Tamil sentence is mostly nominative, although there are constructions with certain verbs that require dative subjects. Tamil has Person, Number and Gender (PNG) agreement.

Tamil is a relatively free word order language, but when it comes to noun phrases and clausal constructions it behaves as a fixed word order language. As in other languages, Tamil also has optional and obligatory parts in the noun phrase. Head noun is obligatory and all other constituents that precede the head noun are optional. Clausal constructions are introduced by non-finite verbs. Other characteristics of Tamil are copula drop, accusative drop, genitive drop, and PRO drop (subject drop). Clausal inversion is one of the characteristics of Tamil.

2.1 Copula Drop

Copula is the verb that links the subject and the object nouns usually in existential sentences. Consider the following example 2.

Ex 2: *athu*   *pazaiya*   *maram.* NULL
    It(PN) old(ADJ) tree(N) (Coupla verb)
    (It is an old tree).

The above example sentence (Ex.2.) does not have a finite verb. The copula verb 'aakum' (is+ past + 3rd person neuter), which is the finite verb for that sentence, is dropped in that sentence.

2.2   Accusative Case Drop

Tamil is a nominative-accusative language. Subject nouns occur with nominative case and the direct object nouns occur with accusative case marker. In certain sentence structures accusative case markers are dropped. Consider the following sentences in exaple.3

Ex3.
raman   pazam   caappittaan.
Raman(N) fruit(N)+(acc) eat(V)+past+3sm
(Raman ate fruits.)

In Ex.3, 'raman' is the subject, 'pazaththai' (fruit,N+Acc) is the direct object and 'eat' is the finite verb. In example Ex.3, the accusative marker is dropped in the object noun 'pazam'.

2.3 Genitive Drop

Genitive drop can be defined as a phenomenon where the genitive case can be dropped from a sentence and the meaning of the sentence remains the same. This phenomenon is common in Tamil. Consider the following example 4.

Ex 4.
ithu   raaman   viitu.
(It)PN   Raman(N)   house(N).
(It is Raman's house.)

In Ex.4, the genitive marker is dropped, in the noun phrase 'raamanutiya viitu' and 'raaman viitu' represents 'raamanutiya viitu' (Raaman's house).

2.4 PRO Drop (Zero Pronouns)

In certain languages, the pronouns are dropped when they are grammatically and pragmatically inferable. This phenomenon of pronoun drop is also mentioned as 'zero pronoun', 'null or zero anaphors', 'Null subject'.

These pose a greater challenge in proper identification of chunk boundaries.

3.   Our Approach

Noun-Noun Anaphora resolution is the task of identifying the referent of the noun which has occurred earlier in the document. In a text, a noun phrase may be repeated as a full noun phrase, partial noun phrase, acronym, or semantically close concepts such as synonyms or superordinates. These noun phrases mostly include named entity such as Individuals, place names, organisations, temporal expression, abbreviation such as 'juun' (Jun), 'nav'(Nov) etc., acronyms such as 'i.na' (U.N), etc., demonstrative noun phrases such as 'intha puththakam' (this book), 'antha kuuttam' (that meeting) etc., and definite descriptions such as denoting phrases. The engine to resolve the noun anaphora is built using Conditional Random Fields (Taku Kudo, 2005) technique.

As a first step we pre-process the text with sentence splitter and tokenizer followed by processing with shallow parsing modules, namely, morphological analyser, Part of Speech tagger, Chunker, and Clause boundary identifier. Following this we enrich the text with Name Entities tagging using Named Entity Recognizer.

We have used a morphological analyser built using rule based and paradigm approach (Sobha et al. 2013). PoS tagger was built using a hybrid approach where the output from Conditional Random Fields technique was smoothened with rules. (Sobha et al. 2016). Clause boundary identifier was built using Conditional Random Fields technique with grammatical rules as features (Ram et al. 2012). Named Entity built using CRFs with post processing rules is used (Malarkodi and Sobha, 2012). Table1 show the precision and recall of these processing modules.

S.No.	Preprocessing Modules	Precision (%)	Recall (%)
1	Morphological Analyser	97.23	95.61
2	Part of Speech tagger	94.92	94.92
3	Chunker	91.89	91.89
4	Named Entity Recogniser	83.86	75.38
5	Clause Boundary Identifier	79.89	86.34

Table 1: Statistics of the Corpus.

We consider the noun anaphor as NP_i and the possible antecedent as NP_j. Unlike pronominal resolution, Noun-Noun anaphora resolution requires features such as similarity between NP_i and NP_j. We consider word, head of the noun phrase, named entity tag and definite description tag, gender, sentence position of the NPs and the distance between the sentences with NP_i and NP_j as features. Features used in Noun-Noun Anaphora Resolution are discussed below.

3.1 Features used for ML

The features used in the CRFs techniques are presented below. The features are divided into two types.

3.1.1 Individual Features

- Single Word: Is NPi a single word; Is NPj a single word

- Multiple Words: Number of Words in NPi; Number of Words in NPj

- PoS Tags: PoS tags of both NPi and NPj.

- Case Marker: Case marker of both NPi and NPj.

- Presence of Demonstrative Pronoun: Check for presence of Demonstrative pronoun in NPi and NPj.

3.1.2 Comparison Features

- Full String Match: Check the root words of both the noun phrase NP_i and NP_j are same.

- Partial String Match: In multi world NPs, calculate the percentage of commonality between the root words of NP_i and NP_j.

- First Word Match: Check for the root word of the first word of both the NP_i and NP_j are same.

- Last Word Match: Check for the root word of last word of both the NP_i and NP_j are same.

- Last Word Match with first Word is a demonstrator: If the root word of the last word is same and if there is a demonstrative pronoun as the first word.

- Acronym of Other: Check NP_i is an acronym of NP_j and vice-versa.

4. Experiment, Results and Evaluation

We have collected 1,000 News articles from Tamil News dailies online versions. The text were scrapped from from the web pages, and fed into sentence splitter, followed by a tokeniser. The sentence splitted and tokenised text is pre-processed with syntactic processing tools namely morphanalyser, POS tagger, chunker, pruner clause boundary identifier. After processing with shallow parsing modules we feed it to Named entity recogniser and the Named entities are identified. The News articles are from Sports, Disaster and General News.

We used a graphical tool, PAlinkA, a highly customisable tool for Discourse Annotation (Orasan, 2003) for annotating the noun-noun anaphors. We have used two tags MARKABLEs and COREF. The basic statistics of the corpus is given in table 2.

S.No	Details of Corpus	Count
1	Number of Web Articles annotated	1,000
2	Number of Sentences	22,382
3	Number of Tokens	272,415
4	Number of Words	227,615

Table 2: Statistics of the Corpus.

S. No.	Task	Precision (%)	Recall (%)	F-Measure (%)
1	Noun-Noun Anaphora Resolution	86.14	66.67	75.16

Table 3: Performance of Noun-Noun Anaphora Resolution

The performance scores obtained are presented in table 3. The engine works with good precision and poor recall. On analysing the output, we could understand two types of errors,1, errors introduced by the pre-processing modules and the intrinsic errors introduced by the Noun-noun anaphora engine. This is presented in table 4.

S. No	Task	Intrinsic Errors of the anaphoric modules (%)	Total Percentage (%) of Error introduced by Preprocessing modules
1	Noun-Noun Anaphora Resolution	17.48	7.36

Table 4: Details of errors

The poor recall is due to engine unable to pick certain anaphoric noun phrase such as definite noun phrases. In table 5, we have given the percentage of error introduced by different pre-processing tasks. We have considered the 7.38% error as a whole and given the percentage of contribution of each of the pre-processing tasks.

In noun-noun anaphora resolution, we consider Named entities, proper nouns, demonstrative nouns, abbreviations,

acronyms, and try to identify their antecedents.

Percentage of error contributed by Each Preprocessing module			
Morphological Analyser (%)	PoS Tagger (%)	Chunker (%)	Named Entity Recogniser (%)
11.56	18.78	36.44	33.22

Table 5: Errors introduced by different pre-processing tasks

This task requires high accuracy of noun phrase chunker and PoS tagger. The errors in chunking and PoS tagging percolates badly, as correct NP boundaries are required for identifying the NP head and correct PoS tags are required for identifying the proper nouns. Errors in chunk boundaries introduce errors in chunk head which results in erroneous noun- noun pairs and correct noun-noun pairs may not be identified. The recall is affected due to the errors in identification of proper noun and NER.

Ex.5.a
aruN   vijay   kapilukku   pathilaaka
Arun(N) vijay(N) Kapli(N)+dat instead

theervu_ceyyappattuLLar.
got_select(V)
(Instead of Kapil, Arun Vijay is selected)

Ex.5.b
vijay   muthalil   kalam   iRangkuvaar.
He(PN) first(N)+loc groud(N) enter(V)+future+3sh
(He will be the opener.)

Ex.5.b has proper noun 'vijay' as the subject of the sentences and it refers to 'aruN vijay' (Arun Vijay), the subject of the sentence Ex.5.a. In Ex.5.a, chunker has tagged 'aruN', 'vijay kapilukku' as two NPs instead of 'aruN vijay' and 'kapilukku'. Pronominal resolution engine has identifies 'aruN' as the referent of 'avar' instead of 'aruN vijay' in Ex.5.a. This is partially correct and full chunk is not identified due to the chunking error.

 Noun-Noun anaphora resolution engine fails to handle definite NPs, as in Tamil we do not have definiteness marker, these NPs occur as common noun. Consider the following discourse.

Ex.6.a
maaNavarkaL   pooRattam   katarkaraiyil
Student(N)+Pl demonstration(N)   beach(N)+Loc

nataththinar.
do(V)+past+3pc
(The students did demonstartions in the beach.)

Ex.6.b
kavalarkaL   maaNavarkaLai kalainthu_cella
Police(N)+Pl students(N)   disperse(V)+INF

ceythanar.
do(V)+past+3pc
(The police made the students to disperse.)

Consider the discourse Ex.6. Here in both the sentences 'maaNavarkaL' (students) has occurred referring to the same entity. But these plural NPs occur as a common nouns and the definiteness is not signalled with any markers. So we have not handled these kinds of definite NPs which occur as common nouns.

Popular names and nicknames pose a challenge in noun-noun anaphora resolution. Consider the following examples; 'Gandhi' was popularly called as 'Mahatma', 'Baapuji' etc. Similarly 'Subhas Chandra bose' was popularly called as 'Netaji', 'Vallabhbhai Patel' was known as 'Iron man of India'. These types of popular names and nick names occur in the text without any prior mention. These popular names, nick names can be inferred by world knowledge or deeper analysis of the context of the current and preceding sentence. Similarly shortening of names such as place names namely 'thanjaavur' (Thanajavur) is called as 'thanjai' (Tanjai), 'nagarkovil' (Nagarkovil) is called as 'nellai' (Nellai), 'thamil naadu' (Tamil Nadu) is called as 'Thamilagam' (Tamilagam) etc introduce challenge in noun-noun anaphora identification. These shortened names are introduced in the text without prior mention. The other challenge is usage of anglicized words without prior mention in the text. Few examples for anglicized words are as follows, 'thiruccirappalli' (Thirucharapalli) is anglicized as 'Tirchy', 'thiruvananthapuram' (Thiuvananthapuram) is anglicized as 'trivandrum', 'uthakamandalam' is anglicized as 'ooty'. Spell variation is one of the challenges in noun-noun anaphora resolution. In News articles, the spell variations are very high, even within the same article. Person name such as 'raaja' (Raja) is also written as 'raaca'. Similarly the place name 'caththiram' (lodge) is also written as 'cathram'. In written Tamil, there is a practice of writing words without using letters with Sanskrit phonemes. This creates a major reason for bigger number of spell variation in Tamil. Consider the words such as 'jagan' (Jagan), 'shanmugam' (Shanmugam), and 'krishna' (Krishna), these words will also be written as 'cagan', 'canmugam' and 'kiruccanan'. These spell variations need to be normalised with spell normalisation module before pre-processing the text.

Spelling variation, Anglicization, Spelling error in NEs lead to errors in correct resolution of noun anaphors. Consider the following example, same entity 'raaja' (Raja) will be written as 'raaja' and 'raaca'.

Due to incorrect chunking, the entities required to form the co-refernce chains are partially identified. Consider example 7.

Ex.7
netharlaanthu aNi,   netharlaanthu, netharlaanthu aNi
Netherland   Team,   Netherland,   Netherland   Team

Consider Ex.7, the same entities as occurred as both 'netharlaanthu aNi' (Netherland Team) and 'netharlaanthu' (Netherland) in the News article. The chunker has wrongly tagged 'netharlaanthu' (Netherland) and 'aNi' (team) as two different chunks. The resultant co-reference chain was 'netharlaanthu', 'netharlaanthu' and 'netharlaanthu'. 'aNi' in both NPs are missed out but to the chunker error.

Similarly in News articles, the place name entities are mentioned as place name or a description referring to the place name. Consider the following examples Ex.8.a, and Ex.8.b.

Ex.8.a
mumbai, inthiyaavin varththaka thalainakaram
Mumbai, India's   Economic Capital

Ex.8.b
kaaci, punitha nakaram
Kasi,   the holy city

In Ex.8.a and Ex.8.b, there are two entities each in both and the NPs refer to the same entity. These kinds of entites are not handled by the Noun-Noun anaphora resolution engine and these entities are missed, while forming the co-reference chain. There are errors in identifying synonymous NP entities as presented in following discourse 9.

Ex.9.a
makkaL   muuththa   kaavalthuRaiyinarootu
People(N) senior(Adj)   police(N)+soc

muRaiyittanar.
argue(V)+past+3p
(People argued with the senior police officer.)

Ex.9.b
antha   athikaariyin   pathiLai eeRRu
That(Det)   officer(N)+gen answer(N) accept(V)+vbp

cenRanar.
go(V)+past+3p
(Accepting the officer's answer they left.)

Consider Ex.9.a and Ex.6.9.b, 'muuththa kaavalthuRaiyinarootu' (Senior police person) in Ex.9.a and 'athikaari' (officer) in Ex.9.b refer to the same entity. For robust Identification of these kinds of synonyms NPs we require synonym dictionaries.

Thus these kinds of noun phrases pose a challenge in resolving noun –noun anaphors.

5.   Conclusion

We have discussed development of noun-noun anaphor resolution in Tamil using Conditional Random Fields, a machine learning technique. We have presented in detail, the characteristics of Tamil, which pose challenges in resolving these noun-noun anaphors. We have presented an in-depth error analysis describing the intrinsic errors in the resolution and the errors introduced by the pre-processing modules.

6.   Bibliographical References

Bengtson, E. & Roth, D. (2008). Understanding the value of features for coreference resolution. In Proceedings of EMNLP, pp. 294-303.

Culotta, A. Wick, M. Hall, R. & McCallum, A. (2007). First-order probabilistic models for coreference resolution. In Proceedings of HLT/NAACL, pp. 81-88.

Halliday, M.A.K. and Hasan, R. (1976). Cohesion in English. Longman Publishers, London.

Malarkodi CS. Pattabhi RK Rao & Sobha Lalitha Devi (2012). Tamil NER – Coping with Real Time Challenges. In Proceedings of Workshop on Machine Translation and Parsing in Indian Languages, COLING 2012, Mumbai, India.

Ng V & Cardie, C(2002). Improving machine learning approaches to coreference resolution. In proceedings of the 40th Annual Meeting of the Association for Computational Linguistics, pp. 104-111.

Bartłomiej Niton, Paweł Morawiecki, and Maiej Ogrodniczuk. (2018). Deep Neural Networks for Coreference Resolution for Polish. In Proceedings of the Eleventh International Conference on Language Resources and Evaluation (LREC) 2018, pp. 395-400.

Raghunathan, K. Lee, H. Rangarajan, S. Chambers, N. Surdeanu, M. Jurafsky, D. & Manning, C. (2010). A multi-pass sieve for coreference resolution. In Proceedings of EMNLP, pp. 492-501.

Rahman, A & Ng, V (2009). Supervised Models for Coreference Resolution. In Proceedings of the Conference on Empirical Methods in Natural Language Processing, pp. 968-977.

Ram, RVS. Bakiyavathi, T. Sindhujagopalan, Amudha, K. & Sobha, L. (2012). Tamil Clause Boundary Identification: Annotation and Evaluation. In the Proceedings of 1st Workshop on Indian Language Data: Resources and Evaluation, Istanbul.

Orasan, C. (2003). PALinkA: A highly customisable tool for discourse annotation. In Proceedings of the 4th SIGdial Workshop on Discourse and Dialogue, ACL'03. pp. 39-43.

Sobha Lalitha Devi, Marimuthu, K. Vijay Sundar Ram, R. Bakiyavathi, T. & Amudha, K (2013). Morpheme Extraction in Tamil using Finite State Machines. In Proceedings of Morpheme Extraction Task at FIRE.

Sobha Lalitha Devi, Pattabhi RK Rao & Vijay Sundar Ram, R (2016). AUKBC Tamil Part-of-Speech Tagger (AUKBC-TamilPoSTagger 2016v1). Web Download. Computational Linguistics Research Group, AU-KBC Research Centre, Chennai, India

Soon WH Ng & Lim, D (2001). A machine learning approach to coreference resolution of noun phrases. Computational Linguistics, vol. 27, no. 4, pp. 521-544.

Taku Kudo (2005). CRF++, an open source toolkit for CRF, http://crfpp.sourceforge.net

Malayalam Speech Corpus: Design and Development for Dravidian Language

Lekshmi.K.R, Jithesh V S, Elizabeth Sherly
Research Scholar, Senior Linguist, Senior Professor
Bharathiar University, IIITM-K, IIITM-K
lekshmi.kr@iiitmk.ac.in, jithesh.vs@iiitmk.ac.in, sherly@iiitmk.ac.in

Abstract
To overpass the disparity between theory and applications in language-related technology in the text as well as speech and several other areas, a well-designed and well-developed corpus is essential. Several problems and issues encountered while developing a corpus, especially for low resource languages. The Malayalam Speech Corpus (MSC) is one of the first open speech corpora for Automatic Speech Recognition (ASR) research to the best of our knowledge. It consists of 250 hours of Agricultural speech data. We are providing a transcription file, lexicon and annotated speech along with the audio segment. It is available in future for public use upon request at "www.iiitmk.ac.in/vrclc/utilities/ml_speechcorpus". This paper details the development and collection process in the domain of agricultural speech corpora in the Malayalam Language.
Keywords: Malayalam, ASR, Agricultural Speech corpus, Narrational and Interview Speech Corpora

1. Introduction

Malayalam is the official language of Kerala, Lakshadweep, and Mahe. From 1330 million people in India, 37 million people speak Malayalam ie; 2.88% of Indians. (Wikipedia contributors, 2020). Malayalam is the youngest of all languages in the Dravidian family. Four or five decades were taken for Malayalam to emerge from Tamil. The development of Malayalam is greatly influenced by Sanskrit also.

In the Automatic Speech Recognition (ASR) area many works are progressing in highly and low-resourced languages. The present speech recognition system has achieved a 'Natural' degree of accuracy mainly in Standard American English (Xiong et al., 2016). The accurate recognition of speech exists only for highly resourced languages. But it is still lagging for "non-native" speakers. To increase the accuracy of such an ASR system the speech data for low- resource language like Malayalam is to be increased.

To encourage the research on speech technology and its related applications in Malayalam, a collection of speech corpus is commissioned and named as Malayalam Speech Corpus (MSC). The corpus consists of the following parts.

- 200 hours of Narrational Speech named NS and

- 50 hours of Interview Speech named IS

The raw speech data is collected from *"Kissan Krishideepam"* an agriculture-based program in Malayalam by the Department of Agriculture, Government of Kerala. The NS is created by making a script during the post-production stage and dubbed with the help of people in different age groups and gender but they are amateur dubbing artists. The speech data is thoughtfully designed - for various applications like code mixed language analysis, Automatic Speech Recognition (ASR) related research, speaker recognition – by considering sociolinguistic variables.

This paper represents the development of Narrational and Interview Speech corpora (NS and IS) collected from native Malayalam speakers. The literature survey of different speech corpora creation is detailed in section 2. Section 3 describes the design and demographics of speech data. The section 4 continues with transcription and section 5 deals with lexicon of the speech data and paper concludes with section 6.

2. Literature Survey

Many languages have developed speech corpus and they are open source too. The English read speech corpus is freely available to download for research purposes (Koh et al., 2019) (Panayotov et al., 2015). Similarly, a database is made available with the collection of TED talks in the English language (Hernandez et al., 2018). Databases are available for Indian languages on free download and a payment basis also. For the Malayalam language-based emotion recognition, a database is available (Rajan et al., 2019).

The corpus collection of low resourced languages is a good initiative in the area of ASR. One of such work is done on Latvian language (Pinnis et al., 2014). They created 100 hours of orthographically transcribed audio data and annotated corpus also. In addition to that a four hours of phonetically transcribed audio data is also available. The authors presented the statistics of speech corpus along with criteria for design of speech corpus.

South Africa has eleven official languages. An attempt is made for the creation of speech corpora on these under resourced languages (Barnard et al., 2014). A collection of more than 50 hours of speech in each language is made available. They validated the corpora by building acoustic and language model using KALDI.

Similarly speech corpora for North-East Indian low-resourced languages is also created (Hernandez et al., 2018). The authors collected speech and text corpora on Assamese, Bengali and Nepali. They conducted a statistical study of the corpora also.

3. The Speech Corpora

A recording studio is setup at our visual media lab with a quiet and sound proof room. A standing microphone is used for recording NS corpora. IS corpora is collected directly from the farmers using recording portable Mic at their place. Hundred speakers are involved in the recording of NS and IS corpora.

3.1. Narrational and Interview Speech Corpora

The written agricultural script, which is phonetically balanced and phonetically rich (up to triphone model), was given to the speakers to record the Narrational Speech. Scripts were different in content. An example script is provided in Fig:1. They were given enough time to record the data. If any recording issues happened, after rectification by the recording assistant it was rerecorded.

പറയാതെ അറിയാം പാലക്കാടാണെന്ന്. ....

കേരളത്തിന്റെ കോട്ടവാതിൽ. ...

ചെന്തമിഴിന്റെ ഈണമുള്ള കാറ്റ വരുന്നുണ്ട്. ....

കരിമ്പനകളിൽ അത് ചൂളം കുത്തിയാടുന്നു. ...

പൊള്ളാച്ചി റോഡിൽ കൊഴിഞ്ഞാം പാറയിലേയ്ക്ക് ഇനിയും ദൂരമുണ്ട്.

പാതയരികിൽ തണൽ മരങ്ങൾ കടവിരിച്ച് നിൽക്കുന്നുണ്ട്.

ഇടത്തേ കാഴ്ചയ്ക്ക് കുളിരായി നീലനിരാളം പുതച്ചുകിടക്കുന്ന സഹ്യൻ.

എങ്കിലും നെട്ടകെ മുറിക്കുന്ന ഊഷരമായ കൃഷിയിടങ്ങൾ പലതുണ്ട് പാലക്കാട്ട്.

കാലിക്കൂട്ടം മേയ്യുന്ന പാടവരമ്പിൽ മനുഷ്യ ജീവിതത്തിന്റെ പ്രയാണങ്ങൾ കാണാം.

Figure 1: Example of script file for dubbing

The Narrational Speech is less expensive than Interview Speech because it is difficult to get data for the ASR system. The IS data is collected in a face-to-face interview style. The literacy and the way to communicate information fluently have given less focus. The interviewee with enough experience in his field of cultivation is asked to speak about his cultivation and its features. The interviewer should be preferably a subject expert in the area of cultivation. Both of them are given separate microphones for this purpose.

Few challenges were faced during the recording of the speech corpus. There were lot of background noise like sounds of vehicles, animals, birds, irrigation motor and wind. Another main issue that happened during post production is the difference in pronunciation styles in the Interview Speech corpora collection. This caused difficulty during validation of the corpus. The recording used to extend up to 5-6 hours depending on speakers. The recorded data is then given for post-production to clean unwanted information from that.

3.2. Speaker Criteria

We have set a few criteria for recording the Narrational Speech data.

- The speakers are at minimum age of 18

- They are citizens of India

- Speakers are residents of Kerala

- The mother tongue of the speaker should be Malayalam without any specific accents

3.3. Recording Specifications

Speech data is collected with two different microphones for NS and IS. For Narrational Speech, Shure SM58-LC cardioid vocal microphone without cable is used. For IS, we utilized Sennheiser XSW 1-ME2-wireless presentation microphone of range 548-572 MHz Steinberg Nuendo and Pro Tools are used for the audio post-production process.

The audio is recorded in 48 kHz sampling frequency and 16 bit sampling rate for broadcasting and the same is down sampled to 16 kHz sampling frequency and 16 bit sampling rate for speech-related research purposes. The recordings of speech corpora are saved in WAV files.

3.4. Demographics

MSC aims to present a good quality audio recording for speech related research. The NS and IS corpus have both male and female speakers. In NS, the male and female speakers are made up with 75% and 25% respectively. IS have more male speakers than females with 82% and 18% of total speakers.The other demographics available from the collected data are Community, Place of Cultivation and Type of Cultivation.

Category	NS (%)	IS (%)
Hindu	85	51
Christian	10	35
Muslim	05	14
Total	100	100

Table 1: Demographic details of speakers by community

Table 2 and 3 contains the details of the place of cultivation and the type of cultivation in Kerala.

Place of Cultivation (District wise)	IS(%)
Thiruvananthapuram	26
Kollam	21
Pathanamthitta	02
Ernakulam	07
Alappuzha	08
Kottayam	08
Idukki	09
Thrissur	12
Wayanad	03
Kozhikode	02
Kannur	02
Total	100

Table 2: Demographic details of speakers by place of cultivation

Type of Cultivation	IS (%)
Animal Husbandry	10
Apiculture	11
Diary	16
Fish and crab farming	05
Floriculture	07
Fruits and vegetables	22
Horticulture	04
Mixed farming	07
Organic farming	08
Poultry	07
Terrace farming	03
Total	100

Table 3: Demographic details of speakers by type of cultivation

4. Transcription

The NS and IS corpora are transcribed orthographically into Malayalam text. The transcribers are provided with the audio segments that the speaker read. Their task is to transcribe the content of the audio into Malayalam and into phonetic text. A sample of three transcribed data with demographic details is shown below and the annotated speech of first two sentences is depicted in Fig 2.

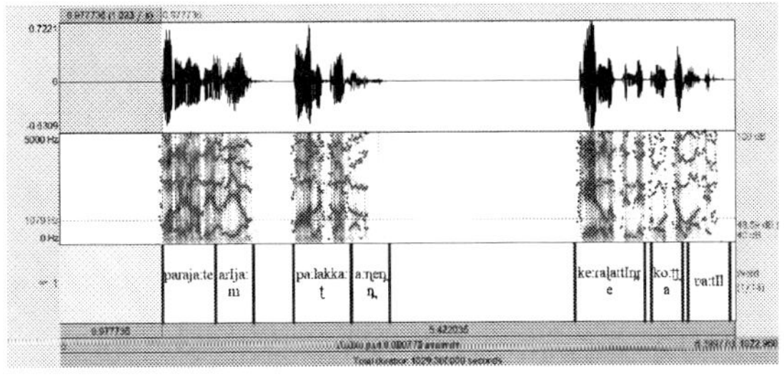

Figure 2: An example of Annotated Speech Corpora

Sample 1: Record Entry No : 180220_01_01

In the first sample a Narrational Speech is detailed. The narrator is about 45 years old and he is describing the details about Palakkad a district in Kerala and a mango estate there. Few sentences are displayed below.

Sentence 1:

പറയാതെ അറിയാം പാലക്കാടാണെന്ന്

paraja:te arIja:m pa:lakka:ʈa:ɳeɳɳ

<Without saying we can understand that it is Palakkad>

Sentence 2:

കേരളത്തിന്റെ കോട്ട വാതിൽ

ke:raɭattIɳre ko:ʈʈa ʋa:tIl

< Kerala's Castle door>

Sentence 3:

സേലവും ധർമ്മപുരിയും കൃഷ്ണഗിരിയുമൊക്കെയാണ് മൽഗോവയുടെ നാടുകൾ

se:laʋʊm dʰarmmapʊrIjʊm kr̥ʂɳagIrIjʊmokkeja:ɳ malgo:ʋajʊʈe ɳa:ʈʊkaɭ

<Selam dharmapuri and krishnagiri are the birthplaces of Malgova>

Sample 2: Record Entry 2: 180220_02_01

The sample shown below is an Interview Speech. The interviewer is an agriculture officer of age 50 and interviewee is the owner of farm about 55 years old.

Sentence 1:

മരുഭൂമിയിൽ നിന്ന് ആഗ്രഹിച്ചതുപോലെയുള്ള കാര്യങ്ങൾ ഇവിടെ ഈ കേരളത്തിലെ ഭൂമിയിൽ വന്നപ്പോൾ സാക്ഷാത്ക്കരിക്കാൻ പറ്റിയെന്നു തോന്നുന്നുണ്ടോ?

marʊbʰu:mIjIl ɳIɳɳ a:grahI̤t̤ʃatʊpo:lejʊɭɭa ka:rjaŋŋaɭ IʋIʈe i: ke:raɭattIle bʰu:mIjIl ʋaɳɳappo:l sa:kʂa:tkkarIkka:ɳ parrIjeɳɳʊ to:ɳɳʊɳɳʊɳʈo:?

<Do you think you could fulfill what you have wished or envisioned from the desert, here in your homeland, Kerala?>

Sentence 2:

തീർച്ചയായിട്ടും, നമ്മൾ ഇവിടെ നമ്മുടെ കൈ കൊണ്ടു വെച്ച് അത് പൂത്ത് അതിന്റെ അകത്ത് നിന്ന് ഒരു മാങ്ങ പറിക്കുക അത് കഴിക്കുക അത് നമ്മുടെ ഏറ്റവും വേണ്ടപ്പെട്ടവർക്ക് കൊടുക്കുക എന്നുള്ളത് സാധിച്ചു.

ti:rʧʧaja:jIʈʈʊm, ᶇammaɭ IʊIʈe ᶇammʊʈe kəɪ konʈʊ
ʋeʧʧ at pu:tt atIᶇre akatt ᶇIᶇᶇ orʊ ma:ᶇᶇa parIkkʊka
at kaˌIkkʊka at ᶇammʊʈe e:rraʋʊm ʋe:ᶇtappeʈʈaʋarkk
koʈʊkkʊka eᶇᶇʊɭɭat sa:dʰIʧʧʊ.

<Definitely we could. What we have planted here by our-
selves blossomed, bore fruit, relished it and shared it with
our dear ones>

5. Lexicon

The pronunciation dictionary, called Lexicon contains a
collection of unique 4925 words. The audio collection process is still going on which will increase the lexicon size.
The lexicon consists of word and its corresponding phone-
mic and syllabic representation as in the example shown in
Fig 3.

Word	Phoneme	Syllable
അത് /at̪/	a t	a t
ഇവിടെ /IʋIʈe/	I ʋ I ʈe	I ʋI ʈe
നാടുകൾ /ᶇa:ʈʊkaɭ/	ᶇ a: ʈ ʊ ka ɭ	ᶇa: ʈʊ ka ɭ
നമ്മുടെ /ᶇammʊʈe/	ᶇ a m m ʊ ʈ e	ᶇa mmʊ ʈe
കഴിക്കുക /kaˌIkkʊka/	K a ˌI k k ʊ k a	Ka ˌI kkʊ ka
പുത്ത് /pu:tt/	p u: t t	pu: tt

Figure 3: Example of the lexicon

6. Conclusion

Speech is the primary and natural mode of communication
than writing. It is possible to extract more linguistic information from speech than text like emotions and accent.
Speech related applications are more useful for illiterate
and old people. The articulatory and acoustic information
can be obtained from a good audio recording environment.
One of the important features of speech data is that, there
is less interference from a second party compared to textual
data.

To encourage the academic research in speech related applications, a good number of multilingual and multipurpose
speech corpora for Indian languages is required. The re-
sponsibility to develop such corpora still lies on the shoul-
der of the concerned researcher. Also the role of language
corpora is very significant to preserve and maintain the linguistic heritage of our country.

The release of MSC will be one of the first speech corpora of Malayalam, contributing 200 hours of Narrational
Speech and 50 hours of Interview Speech data for public
use. The lexicon and annotated speech is also made available with the data. Future work includes creation of corpora
related to tourism and entertainment domains and enhance-
ment of quality of speech by building an ASR using KALDI
toolkit. The updates on corpus will be accessible through
"www.iiitmk.ac.in/vrclc/utilities/ml_speechcorpus".

Acknowledgements

This research is supported by the Kerala State Council for
Science, Technology and Environment (KSCSTE). I thank
KSCSTE for funding the project under the Back-to-lab
scheme. I also thank Agri team, Indian Institute of Information Technology and Management-Kerala, Kissan Project
for collecting the audio data.

Bibliographical References

Barnard, E., Davel, M. H., van Heerden, C., De Wet, F., and
Badenhorst, J. (2014). The nchlt speech corpus of the
south african languages. In *Workshop Spoken Language
Technologies for Under-resourced Languages (SLTU)*.

Hernandez, F., Nguyen, V., Ghannay, S., Tomashenko, N.,
and Estève, Y. (2018). Ted-lium 3: twice as much data
and corpus repartition for experiments on speaker adaptation. In *International Conference on Speech and Computer*, pages 198–208. Springer.

Koh, J. X., Mislan, A., Khoo, K., Ang, B., Ang, W., Ng, C.,
and Tan, Y.-Y. (2019). Building the singapore english
national speech corpus. *Malay*, 20(25.0):19–3.

Panayotov, V., Chen, G., Povey, D., and Khudanpur, S.
(2015). Librispeech: an asr corpus based on public domain audio books. In *2015 IEEE International Conference on Acoustics, Speech and Signal Processing
(ICASSP)*, pages 5206–5210. IEEE.

Pinnis, M., Auzina, I., and Goba, K. (2014). Designing
the latvian speech recognition corpus. In *LREC*, pages
1547–1553.

Rajan, R., Haritha, U., Sujitha, A., and Rejisha, T. (2019).
Design and development of a multi-lingual speech corpora (tamar-emodb) for emotion analysis. *Proc. Inter-
speech 2019*, pages 3267–3271.

Wikipedia contributors. (2020). Malayalam — Wikipedia,
the free encyclopedia. [Online; accessed 21-February-
2020].

Xiong, W., Droppo, J., Huang, X., Seide, F., Seltzer, M.,
Stolcke, A., Yu, D., and Zweig, G. (2016). Achiev-
ing human parity in conversational speech recognition.
arXiv preprint arXiv:1610.05256.

Proceedings of the WILDRE5– 5th Workshop on Indian Language Data: Resources and Evaluation, pages 29–32
Language Resources and Evaluation Conference (LREC 2020), Marseille, 11–16 May 2020
© European Language Resources Association (ELRA), licensed under CC-BY-NC

Multilingual Neural Machine Translation involving Indian Languages

Pulkit Madaan, Fatiha Sadat
IIIT Delhi, UQAM
Delhi India, Montreal Canada
pulkit16257@iiitd.ac.in, sadat.fatiha@uqam.ca

Abstract

Neural Machine Translations (NMT) models are capable of translating a single bilingual pair and require a new model for each new language pair. Multilingual Neural Machine Translation models are capable of translating multiple language pairs, even pairs which it hasn't seen before in training. Availability of parallel sentences is a known problem in machine translation. Multilingual NMT model leverages information from all the languages to improve itself and performs better. We propose a data augmentation technique that further improves this model profoundly. The technique helps achieve a jump of more than 15 points in BLEU score from the Multilingual NMT Model. A BLEU score of 36.2 was achieved for Sindhi–English translation, which is higher than any score on the leaderboard of the LoResMT SharedTask at MT Summit 2019, which provided the data for the experiments.

Keywords: Neural Machine Translation, Low Resource Languages, Multilingual Transformer, Deep Learning, End-to-end Learning, Data Augmentation, Transfer Learning

1. Introduction

A lot of the models for end-to-end NMT are trained for single language pairs. Google's Multilingual NMT (Johnson et al., 2017) is a single model capable of translating to and from many languages. The model is fed a token identifying a target language uniquely along with the source language sentence. This allows the model to translate between pairs for which the model hasn't seen parallel data, essentially zero-shot translations. The model is also able to improve upon individual translation qualities too by the help of other languages. NMT suffers from the lack of data. And as Arivazhagan et al.(2019b) and Koehn et al.(2017) too recognize, lack of data makes NMT a non-trivial challenge for low-resource languages. Multilingual NMT is a step towrds solving this problem which leverages data from other language pairs and does an implicit transfer learning. We propose to improve this quality further with a data-augmentation technique that was able to improve the BLEU scores two fold in our experiments. The technique is simple and can work with any model. We show that increasing the amount of data available for training artificially with our technique in a way as simple as just swapping the source with target sentences and using the same sentence as source and target can improve the BLEU scores significantly. Also, we show that since all language pairs share the same encoder and the same decoder, in a case of transfer learning, the model is able to leverage data from rich resource language pairs for learning better translations for low-resource pairs. Using Hindi–English data in training improved the BLEU scores for {Bhojpuri, Sindhi, Magahi}<>English. The structure of the present paper is described as follows: Section 2 presents the state of the art. Section 3 presents our proposed methodology. Section 4 describes the corpora used in this research. In section 5, we put forward our experiments and evaluations, perform an ablative analysis and compare our system's performance with other Google's Neural Machine Translation(Johnson et al., 2017). Section 6, compares our results with other methods that participated in the LoResMT Shared Task(Karakanta et al., 2019) at the MT Summit 2019. Finally in Section 7, we state our conclusions and perspectives for future research.

2. Related Work

Significant progress has been made in end-to-end NMT (Cho et al., 2014; Sutskever et al., 2014; Bahdanau et al., 2015) and some work has been done to adapt it to a multilingual setting. But, before the mulitilingual approach of Johnson et al., 2017, none of the approaches have a single model capable of dealing with multiple language pairs in a many-to-many setting. Dong et al.(2015) use different decoders and attention layers for different target languages. Firat et al.(2016) use a shared attention layer but an encoder per source language and a decoder per target language. Lee et al.(2017) use a single model with the whole model shared across all pairs but it can only be used for a single target language. The model proposed by Johnson et al.(2017) has a single model for a many-to-many task and is able to perform in zero-shot setting too wher it can translate sentences between pairs whose parallel data wasn't seen by the model during training. Arivazhagan et al.(2019a) also propose a model for zero-shot translation that improves upon Google's Multilingual NMT Model (Johnson et al., 2017) and achieves results on par with pivoting. They propose English as the pivot language and feed the target language token to the decoder instead of the encoder. In order to improve the independence of encoder on source language they maximise the similarity between all sentence vectors and their English parallel sentence embeddings and minimize the translation cross-entropy loss. They use a discriminator and train the encoder adversarially for similarity maximisation. Artetxe et al.(2018) and Yang et al.(2018) also train the encoder adversarially to learn a shared latent space. There has been a lot of work done to improve NMT models using data augmentation. Sennrich et al (2016a) proposed automatic back-translation to augment the dataset. But, as mentioned in SwitchOut (Wang et al., 2018) faces challenges in initial models. Fadaee et al.(2017) propose

Augment	Source		Target	
Forward	That town is two miles away.	[English]	वह नगर दो मील की दूरी पर है।	[Hindi]
Backward	वह नगर दो मील की दूरी पर है।	[Hindi]	That town is two miles away.	[English]
Self	That town is two miles away.	[English]	That town is two miles away.	[English]
Self	वह नगर दो मील की दूरी पर है।	[Hindi]	वह नगर दो मील की दूरी पर है।	[Hindi]
High	Is everybody busy?	[English]	Tout le monde est-il occupé ?	[French]

Figure 1: An example of different augments. Here the low resource pair of languages is English–Hindi, and the high resource pair language set is English–French

a data augmentation technique where they synthesise new data by replacing a common word in the source sentence with a rare word and the corresponding word in the target sentence with its translation. And to maintain the syntactic validity of the sentence, they use an LSTM language model. Zhu et al.(2019) propose a method in which they obtain parallel sentences from multilingual websites. They scrape the websites to get monolingual data on which they learn word embeddings. These embeddings are used to induce a bilingual lexicon and then use a trained model to identify parallel sentences. Ours is a much simpler way, which does not require an additional model, is end-to-ed trainable and is still at par with some Statistical Machine Translation methods submitted at the SharedTask.

3. The Proposed Methodology

The technique we propose is simple consists of four components named **Forward**, **Backward**, **Self** and **High**. **Forward** augmentation is the given data itself. **Backward** augmentation is generated by switching the source and target label in the **Forward** Data, so the source sentence becomes the target sentence and vice versa in parallel sentence pair. **Self** augmentation is generated by using only the required language from the parallel sentences and cloning them as their own target sentences, so the source and target sentence are the same. An example of the augmentations is shown in Figure 1. We know that translation models improve with increase in data and since we also have the same encoder for every language, we can use a language pair that is similar to the language pairs of the task and is a high resource pair to further improve the encoder in encoding source independent embeddings, for transfer learning through the Multilingual architecture of Johnson et al.(2017) . So we propose **Multilingual+** which uses the above mentioned three augmentations (Forward, Backward, Self) along with **High** augmentation; **High** augmentation consists of high-resource language pairs, like Hindi–English parallel data, in Forward, Backward and Self augmentations. This helps in improving the translation models of low resource pairs; {Bhojpuri, Sindhi, Magahi}<>English.

4. Dataset

Parallel data from four different language pairs are used in the experiments. Following are the language pairs along with the number of parallel sentences of each pair:

1. Sindhi–English (29,014)

2. Magahi–English (3,710)

3. Bhojpuri–English (28,999)

4. Hindi–English (1,561,840)

Data for pairs 1–3 were made available at the Shared Task at MT Summit 2019. While data for pair 4 was obtained from the IIT Bombay English–Hindi Corpus (Kunchukuttan et al., 2018). The Train-Val-Test splits were used as given by the respective data providers.

5. Experiments

We performed experiments on the Multingual+ model and showed how the addition of each of augmentations we proposed improves the performance by an ablative analysis. After augmentation, the source sentences get a target language token prepended. Joint Byte-Pair Encoding is learnt for subword segmentation (Sennrich et al., 2016b) to address the problem of rare words. Byte-Pair encoding was learnt over the training data and was used to segment subwords for both the training and the test data. A Joint dictionary was learnt over all the languages. This is the only pre-processing that we do besides the augmentation. The basic architecture is the same as in Johnson et al.(2017). A single encoder and decoder shared over all the languages. Adam (Kingma and Ba, 2015) optimizer was use, with initial beta values of 0.9 and 0.98 along with label smoothing and dropout(0.3). Following are the augmentations included in Multinlingual+

- **Forward**
  Sindhi-to-English, Bhojpuri-to-English, Magahi-to-English

- **Backward**
  English-to-Sindhi, English-to-Bhojpuri, English-to-Magahi

- **Self**
  Sindhi-to-Sindhi, Bhojpuri-to-Bhojpuri, Magahi-to-Magahi, English-to-English

- **High**
  Hindi-to-English, English-to-Hindi, Hindi-to-Hindi

	Sin-to-Eng	Eng-to-Sin	Bho-to-Eng	Eng-to-Bho	Mag-to-Eng	Eng-to-Mag
Base	15.74*	–	6.11*	–	2.46*	–
Base + Back	18.09*	11.38*	5.01*	0.2	2.55*	0.2
Base + Back + Self	30.77*	18.98*	7.38*	0.6	4.61*	1.2
†**Multilingual+**	**36.2**	**28.8**	**15.6**	**3.7**	**13.3**	**3.5**

Table 1: BLEU scores of different language pairs and directions in the different experiments.
*Results on test data evaluated by the Shared Task at MT Summit 2019 committee.
† Not submitted for the SharedTask

To understand how each augmentation improves the BLEU score, we create 4 methods:

- **Base**
  This is the standard model as used in (Johnson et al., 2017), hence it uses only **Forward** and forms our baseline.

- **Base + Back**
  We add **Backward** augmentation to the baseline model

- **Base + Back + Self**
  We add **Self** & **Backward** augmentation to the baseline.

- **Multilingual+**
  This uses all the augmentations:**High** along with **Forward**, **Backward** & **Self**.

Parameters and training procedures are set as in Johnson et al.(2017). PyTorch Sequence-to-Sequence library, **fairseq** (Ott et al., 2019), was used to run the experiments. Table 1 shows that **Multilingual+** consistently outperforms the others. The table also confirms that the more augmentations you add to the Multilingual NMT model (Johnson et al., 2017), the more it improves. Adding **Backward**, then **Self** and then a new language pair improved the results at each level. All the BLEU scores reported, except star (*) marked, are calculated using SacreBLEU (Post, 2018) on the development set provided.

6. Comparisons

We compared our results with other models submitted at the LoResMT Shared Task at the MT Summit 2019. The submission to the Shared Task followed a naming convention to distinguish between different types of corpora used, which we will follow too. The different types of corpora and their abbreviations are as follows:

- Only the provided parallel corpora [-a]

- Only the provided parallel and monolingual corpora [-b]

Using these abbreviations the methods were named in the following manner"

<TeamCode>-<Language-and-Direction>-
<MethodName>-<Used-Corpora-Abbreviation>

Our Team Code was L19T3 and we submitted Base (as Method_1), Base+Back (as Method_2) and Base+Back+Self (as Method_3) all under -a category. Multilingual+ was developed later. Table 2 shows the top 3 performers in different translation directions along with Multilingual+. Method3-b from team L19T2 is a Phrase Based Statistical Machine Translation model. While their Method2-a is an NMT model that uses a sequence-to-sequence approach along with self-attention. pbmt-a model from team L19T5 is again a Phrase Based Statistical Machine Translation model. While their xform-a model is an NMT model. Both of the NMT models of the other teams train a different model for different language pairs, one for each, while ours is a one for all model. Multilingual+ is the best performer in Sin-to-Eng and Mag-to-Eng task, second best performer in Eng-to-Sin and Bho-to-Eng tasks. These results show the superiority of our simple approach. Our data augmentation technique is comparable or better than the best of the methods on the leaderboard of the SharedTask.

In Eng-to-Sin task L19T2-Eng2Sin-Method3-b scores the best while the second best is Multinlingual+. This could be because the former is a Statistical Machine Translation Model. Though, it surpasses the L19T2's NMT model. For Bho-to-Eng it is able to surpass pbmt-a of team L19T5 it still lags behind their NMT model. This can be explained as we have more data for Sindhi than Bhojpuri and though we were able to improve the performance by augmenting data, it still remains behind statistical machine translation approach of L19T2. The success of our simple approach can be attributed to its conjunction with Multilingual NMT. Multilingual NMT is able to use data of all languages to improve them all together, and by even further increasing this data, we improve the model greatly.

7. Conclusion and Future Work

We have presented a simple data augmentation technique coupled with a multilingual transformer that gives a jump of 15 points in BLEU score without any new data and 20 points in BLEU score if a rich resource language pair is introduced, over a standard multilingual transformer. It performs at par or better than best models submitted at the Shared Task. This demonstrates that a multilingual transformer is sensitive to the amount of data used and a simple augmentation technique like ours can provide a significant boost in BLEU scores. Back-translation (Sennrich et al., 2016a) can be coupled with our approach to experiment and analyse the effectiveness of this amalgam.

Rank	Sin-to-Eng		Eng-to-Sin	
1	L19T2-Sin2Eng-Method3-b	31.32	L19T2-Eng2Sin-Method3-b	**37.58**
2	Base+Back+Self	30.77	L19T2-Eng2Sin-Method2-a	25.17
3	L19T5-sin2eng-xform-a	28.85	Base+Back+Self	18.98
	Multilingual+	**36.2**	Multilingual+	28.8

Rank	Bho-to-Eng		Mag-to-Eng	
1	L19T2-Bho2Eng-Method3-b	**17.03**	L19T2-Mag2Eng-Method3-b	9.71
2	L19T5-bho2eng-xform-a	15.19	L19T5-mag2eng-pbmt-a	5.64
3	L19T5-bho2eng-pbmt-a	14.2	Base+Back+Self	4.61
	Multilingual+	15.6	Multilingual+	**13.3**

Table 2: Top 3 performers in LoResMT Shared Task in different translation directions along with Multilingual+

8. Bibliographical References

Arivazhagan, N., Bapna, A., Firat, O., Aharoni, R., Johnson, M., and Macherey, W. (2019a). The missing ingredient in zero-shot neural machine translation. *CoRR*, abs/1903.07091.

Arivazhagan, N., Bapna, A., Firat, O., Lepikhin, D., Johnson, M., Krikun, M., Chen, M. X., Cao, Y., Foster, G., Cherry, C., Macherey, W., Chen, Z., and Wu, Y. (2019b). Massively multilingual neural machine translation in the wild: Findings and challenges. *CoRR*, abs/1907.05019.

Artetxe, M., Labaka, G., Agirre, E., and Cho, K. (2017). Unsupervised neural machine translation. *CoRR*, abs/1710.11041.

Bahdanau, D., Cho, K., and Bengio, Y. (2015). Neural machine translation by jointly learning to align and translate. *CoRR*, abs/1409.0473.

Cho, K., van Merrienboer, B., Çaglar Gülçehre, Bougares, F., Schwenk, H., and Bengio, Y. (2014). Learning phrase representations using rnn encoder-decoder for statistical machine translation. *ArXiv*, abs/1406.1078.

Dong, D., Wu, H., He, W., Yu, D., and Wang, H. (2015). Multi-task learning for multiple language translation. In *ACL*.

Fadaee, M., Bisazza, A., and Monz, C. (2017). Data augmentation for low-resource neural machine translation. In *Proceedings of the 55th Annual Meeting of the Association for Computational Linguistics (Volume 2: Short Papers)*, pages 567–573, Vancouver, Canada, July. Association for Computational Linguistics.

Firat, O., Cho, K., and Bengio, Y. (2016). Multi-way, multilingual neural machine translation with a shared attention mechanism. *ArXiv*, abs/1601.01073.

Johnson, M., Schuster, M., Le, Q. V., Krikuna, M., Wu, Y., Chen, Z., Thorat, N., Viégas, F. B., Wattenberg, M., Corrado, G. S., Hughes, M., and Dean, J. (2017). Google's multilingual neural machine translation system: Enabling zero-shot translation. *Transactions of the Association for Computational Linguistics*, 5:339–351.

Alina Karakanta, et al., editors. (2019). *Proceedings of the 2nd Workshop on Technologies for MT of Low Resource Languages*, Dublin, Ireland, August. European Association for Machine Translation.

Kingma, D. P. and Ba, J. (2015). Adam: A method for stochastic optimization. In *3rd International Conference on Learning Representations, ICLR 2015, San Diego, CA, USA, May 7-9, 2015, Conference Track Proceedings*.

Kunchukuttan, A., Mehta, P., and Bhattacharyya, P. (2018). The IIT bombay english-hindi parallel corpus. *Language Resources and Evaluation Conference*, 10.

Lee, J. D., Cho, K., and Hofmann, T. (2017). Fully character-level neural machine translation without explicit segmentation. *Transactions of the Association for Computational Linguistics*, 5:365–378.

Ott, M., Edunov, S., Baevski, A., Fan, A., Gross, S., Ng, N., Grangier, D., and Auli, M. (2019). fairseq: A fast, extensible toolkit for sequence modeling. In *Proceedings of NAACL-HLT 2019: Demonstrations*.

Post, M. (2018). A call for clarity in reporting BLEU scores. In *Proceedings of the Third Conference on Machine Translation: Research Papers*, pages 186–191, Belgium, Brussels, October. Association for Computational Linguistics.

Sennrich, R., Haddow, B., and Birch, A. (2016a). Improving neural machine translation models with monolingual data. *ArXiv*, abs/1511.06709.

Sennrich, R., Haddow, B., and Birch, A. (2016b). Neural machine translation of rare words with subword units. In *Proceedings of the 54th Annual Meeting of the Association for Computational Linguistics (Volume 1: Long Papers)*, pages 1715–1725, Berlin, Germany, August. Association for Computational Linguistics.

Sutskever, I., Vinyals, O., and Le, Q. V. (2014). Sequence to sequence learning with neural networks. In *NIPS*.

Wang, X., Pham, H., Dai, Z., and Neubig, G. (2018). SwitchOut: an efficient data augmentation algorithm for neural machine translation. In *Proceedings of the 2018 Conference on Empirical Methods in Natural Language Processing*, pages 856–861, Brussels, Belgium, October-November. Association for Computational Linguistics.

Yang, Z., Chen, W., Wang, F., and Xu, B. (2018). Unsupervised neural machine translation with weight sharing. *CoRR*, abs/1804.09057.

Proceedings of the WILDRE5– 5th Workshop on Indian Language Data: Resources and Evaluation, pages 33–38
Language Resources and Evaluation Conference (LREC 2020), Marseille, 11–16 May 2020
© European Language Resources Association (ELRA), licensed under CC-BY-NC

Universal Dependency Treebanks for Low-Resource Indian Languages: The Case of Bhojpuri

Atul Kr. Ojha, Daniel Zeman
Charles University, Faculty of Mathematics and Physics
Institute of Formal and Applied Linguistics
shashwatup9k@gmail.com, zeman@ufal.mff.cuni.cz

Abstract

This paper presents the first dependency treebank for Bhojpuri, a resource-poor language that belongs to the Indo-Aryan language family. The objective behind the Bhojpuri Treebank (BHTB) project is to create a substantial, syntactically annotated treebank which not only acts as a valuable resource in building language technological tools, also helps in cross-lingual learning and typological research. Currently, the treebank consists of 4,881 annotated tokens in accordance with the annotation scheme of Universal Dependencies (UD). A Bhojpuri tagger and parser were created using machine learning approach. The accuracy of the model is 57.49% UAS, 45.50% LAS, 79.69% UPOS accuracy and 77.64% XPOS accuracy. The paper describes the details of the project including a discussion on linguistic analysis and annotation process of the Bhojpuri UD treebank.
Keywords: Bhojpuri, Indian languages, parser, low-resource languages, Universal Dependencies, UDPipe

1. Introduction

Bhojpuri is an Indian language that belongs to the Indo-Aryan language group. It is spoken in the western part of Bihar, north-western part of Jharkhand, and the Purvanchal region of Uttar Pradesh. The number of speakers according to the present Census of India[1] is considerably large at 50,579,447. It should be noted that Bhojpuri is spoken not just in India but also in other countries such as Nepal, Trinidad, Mauritius, Guyana, Suriname, and Fiji (Verma, 2003; Ojha, 2019). Since Bhojpuri was considered a dialect of Hindi for a long time, it did not attract much attention from linguists and hence remains among the many lesser known and less-resourced languages of India.

With the rise in language technology for Indian languages, significant developments have been achieved in major Indian languages but contributions towards research in the lesser-known/low-resourced languages remain minimal. Most parsers and treebanks have been developed for the scheduled (official) languages; the non-scheduled and lesser known languages still have a long way to go. In its endevour to fill this gap, the present paper discusses the creation and development of Bhojpuri Universal Dependency (UD) treebank and parser. UD has been acknowledged as an emerging framework for cross-linguistically consistent grammatical annotation. There is an open community with over 300 contributors, who have produced 157 treebanks in 90 languages to date (as per the latest release of UD–v2.5[2] (Zeman et al., 2019). The primary aim of this project is to facilitate multilingual parser development. The system will also take into account cross-lingual learning and perform parsing research from the perspective of language typology. The syntactic part of the annotation scheme can be seen as an evolution of (universal) Stanford dependencies (De Marneffe et al., 2006; De Marneffe and Manning, 2008; De Marneffe et al., 2014), while the lexical and morphological part builds on the Google universal part-of-speech tags (Petrov et al., 2012), and the Interset Interlingua (Zeman, 2008) for morpho-syntactic tagsets.

Section 2. discusses the language resources that have been created so far for the Bhojpuri language. While Bhojpuri has some considerable efforts in progress, it has no dependency treebank and parser. Section 3. discusses methodology to develop the Bhojpuri treebank. Section 4. presents a linguistic study and annotation of the Bhojpuri Dependency treebank while Sections 5. and 6. discuss the development of the Bhojpuri parser and evaluate its results. The final section ends with concluding remarks and future work.

2. Literature Review

In 2013, a consortium was formed under the leadership of IIIT Hyderabad to start a project sponsored by TDIL, Government of India, and called The Development of Dependency Treebank for Indian Languages.[3] The fundamental objective of this project was to resurrect annotation work towards monolingual and parallel treebanks for languages such as Hindi, Marathi, Bengali, Kannada, and Malayalam. To accomplish this treebank model, the Pāṇinian Kāraka Dependency annotation scheme was followed (Bharati et al., 2006). The annotation scheme was previously also utilized to annotate data in Telugu, Urdu, and Kashmiri (Begum et al., 2008; Husain et al., 2010; Bhat, 2017).

Within the Universal Dependencies framework, as of UD release 2.5, treebanks and parsers are available for Sanskrit, Hindi, Urdu, Marathi, Tamil, and Telugu (Zeman et al., 2019; Ravishankar, 2017; Straka and Straková, 2019).

---

[1]http://www.censusindia.gov.in/2011Census/C-16_25062018_NEW.pdf

[2]https://universaldependencies.org/

[3]http://meity.gov.in/content/language-computing-group-vi

NLP research in Bhojpuri has led to the development of a statistical POS tagger (Ojha et al., 2015; Singh and Jha, 2015), a machine-readable dictionary (Ojha, 2016), a language identification tool (Kumar et al., 2018), a Sanskrit-Bhojpuri machine translation system (Sinha and Jha, 2018), and more recently an English-Bhojpuri machine translation system (Ojha, 2019). Nevertheless, there is no prior work on Bhojpuri treebanking and parsing.

3. Data and Methodology

The data for the treebank has been extracted from the Bhojpuri Language Technological Resources (BHLTR) project[4] (Ojha, 2019). The data has been selected from the news and non-fiction domains. For this project, we use 5000 sentences (105,174 tokens) which were previously annotated with part-of-speech tags now used for language-specific tags representation in the XPOS. Out of 5000 sentences and 105,174 tokens, 254 sentences and 4881 tokens have been manually annotated at present, and released in UD 2.5.

The Bhojpuri Treebank (BHTB)[5] follows the annotation guidelines of Universal Dependencies for part-of-speech categories, morphological features, and dependency relations. Since Bhojpuri is closely related to Hindi and there is already a Hindi treebank in UD, we followed the Hindi tagset wherever possible. Besides, the universal part-of-speech tagset (UPOS), UD also permits a secondary tagset (XPOS), which is language-specific and typically follows an established pre-UD practice. We use the Bureau of Indian Standards (BIS) POS tagset[6] here. This is a generic tagset for annotating Indian languages. The XPOS tags were already present in our input data and we obtained the UPOS tags through automatic conversion from XPOS. In addition to UPOS, we use 16 lexical and inflectional features defined in UD. The details of used morphological features, UPOS tags and UD relations and their statistics are demonstrated in Tables 1, 2 and 3.

4. Linguistic Analysis of Bhojpuri Dependency Treebank

As discussed earlier, we followed UD v2 guidelines to annotate BHTB. We mention below some Bhojpuri constructions and their linguistics analysis under UD.

- **Nominal Predicate with Copula**
  Figure 1 is an example of a nominal predicate with a copula. In the example, the copula हS *(ha)* is preceded by the nominal predicate देश *(deśa)*. In accordance with UD, the nominal देश is the root of the sentence and the verbal copula हS is attached to it via the relation cop, as shown in the figure.

Morph. Features	Description	Count
AdpType	Adposition type	726
Aspect	Aspect	242
Case	Case	3007
Echo	Echo word or a reduplicative	9
Foreign	Foreign word	5
Gender	Gender	2916
Mood	Mood	37
Number	Number	3144
NumType	Numeral type	84
Person	Person	2485
Polite	Politeness	103
Poss	Possessive	1
PronType	Pronominal type	163
VerbForm	Form of verb or deverbative	293
Voice	Voice	231

Table 1: Statistics of morphological features used in the BHTB

UPOS Tags	Description	Count
ADJ	Adjective	183
ADP	Adposition	720
ADV	Adverb	18
AUX	Auxiliary	256
CCONJ	Coordinating conjunction	112
DET	Determiner	256
INTJ	Interjection	4
NOUN	Noun	1361
NUM	Numeral	110
PART	Particle	135
PRON	Pronoun	230
PROPN	Proper noun	352
PUNCT	Punctuation	504
SCONJ	Subordinating conjunction	86
VERB	Verb	553
X	Other	1

Table 2: Statistics of UPOS tags used in the BHTB

- **Verbal Predicates**
  We discuss three types of verbal predicates in this section: a simple verb construction, a conjunct verb construction and a compound verb construction. A simple verb or a verb with auxiliary is called simple verb construction. An example is given in Figure 2 where a verb गइल *(gaila)* is combined with an auxiliary रहन *(rahana)*. In UD, the verb is tagged as the root of the sentence and the auxiliary is related to it via the relation aux. In Figure 3, the sentence has both a conjunct verb and a compound verb. The conjunct verb is formed by combining a noun नजर *(najara)* with the compound verb चलि गइल *(cali gaila)*. Moreover, the compound verb is formed by combining

---

[4]https://github.com/shashwatup9k/bho-resources
[5]https://github.com/UniversalDependencies/UD_Bhojpuri-BHTB
[6]http://tdil-dc.in/tdildcMain/articles/134692Draft%20POS%20Tag%20standard.pdf

UD Relations	Description	Count
acl	Clausal modifier of noun	82
advcl	Adverbial clausal modifier	57
advmod	Adverbial modifier	11
amod	Adjectival modifier of noun	160
aux	Auxiliary verb	224
case	Case marker	661
cc	Coordinating conjunction	15
ccomp	Clausal complement	46
clf	Classifier	3
compound	Compound	1191
conj	Non-first conjunct	96
cop	Copula	2
csubj	Clausal subject	9
dep	Unspecified dependency	11
det	Determiner	118
discourse	Discourse element	7
fixed	Non-first word of fixed expression	9
flat	Non-first word of flat structure	1
goeswith	Non-first part of broken word	1
iobj	Indirect object	18
list	List item	10
mark	Subordinating marker	89
nmod	Nominal modifier of noun	678
nsubj	Nominal subject	192
nummod	Numeric modifier	41
obj	Direct object	93
obl	Oblique nominal	245
punct	Punctuation	504
root	Root	254
xcomp	Open clausal complement	55

Table 3: UD relations used in BHTB. Out of 37 relations defined in the UD guidelines, we currently use 30

the main verb चलि *(cali)* with the light verb गइल *(gaila)*. In UD, the main verb चलि is marked as root and the noun नजर is related to it via the compound relation. The light verb गइल, on the other hand, is related to the main verb via the relation aux.

- **Coordination**
  Figure 4 illustrates an example of a coordinate construction. The conjuncts आई *(āīṃ)* and सपरिवार आई *(saparivāra āīṃ)* are conjoined through the conjunction आ *(ā)*. In UD, the first conjunct serves as the technical head and the second conjunct is attached to it via the relation conj. The coordinating conjunction आ is related to the following conjunct via the relation cc.

- **Types of Clauses**
  In UD, subordinate clauses are sub-categorised in five types: clausal subject (csubj), clausal

complement (ccomp), open clausal complement (xcomp), adverbial clausal modifier (advcl), clausal modifier of noun (acl). We found all five types of clauses in Bhojpuri. We demonstrate here an example of a clausal modifier of noun. In Figure 5, the clause जवना के सभे आनन्द लिहल *(javana ke sabhe ānanda lihala)* is a modifier of the noun गवनई *(gavanaī)* which is shown by the tag acl. Interestingly, the clausal modifier is displaced from its base position and right adjoined to the verb. This is a common property of many Indo-Aryan languages.

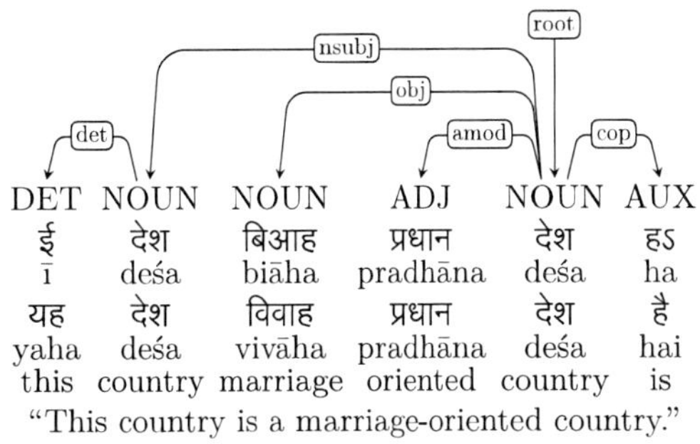

Figure 1: A parallel copular sentence in Bhojpuri (lines 2–3) and Hindi (lines 4–5).

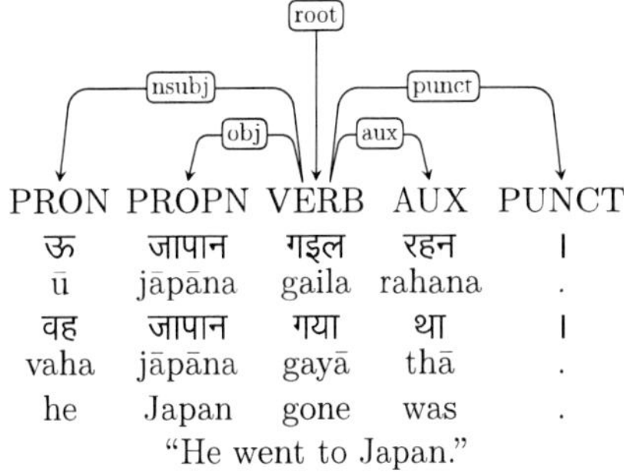

Figure 2: A parallel sentence with simple verb construction in Bhojpuri (lines 2–3) and Hindi (lines 4–5)

5. Development of a Bhojpuri Parser

Initially, we conducted an experiment where the parser was trained on the Hindi UD treebank (HDTB) and applied to Bhojpuri. While the parsing quality suffers from the differences between the two languages, this is partially counterbalanced by the fact that the Hindi treebank is large: there are 16,647 training sentences (351,704 tokens). This experiment was evaluated on the first 50 manually annotated sentences (650 tokens) in Bhojpuri. We found that the Hindi parser gives only 56.77% UAS, 45.61% LAS, and 52.35% UPOS tagging accuracy, respectively (as shown in Table 4). Along with this, the tokenization accuracy of the Hindi model is only 89.15%.

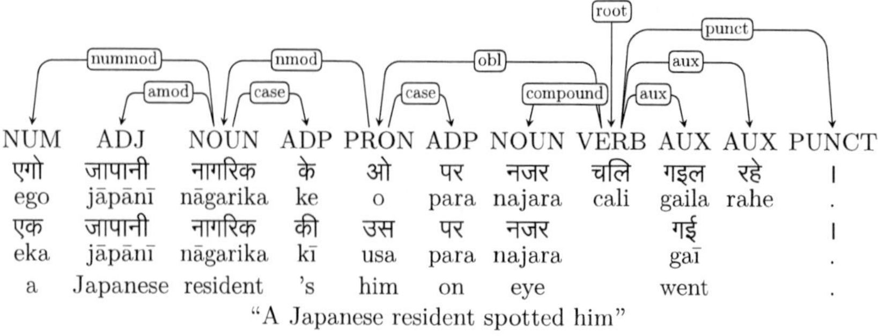

Figure 3: A parallel sentence with compound verb construction in Bhojpuri (lines 2–3) and Hindi (lines 4–5)

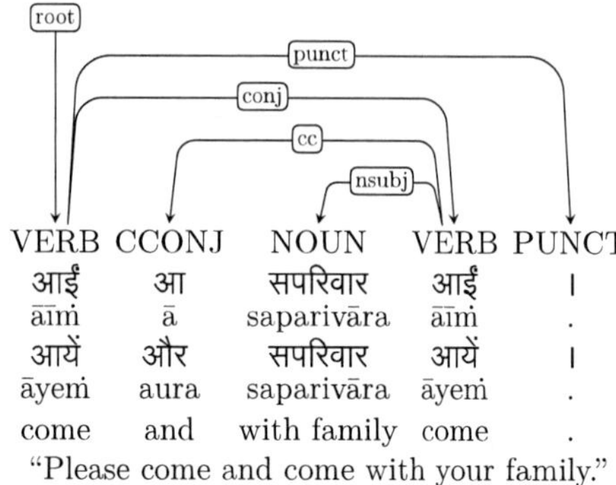

Figure 4: A parallel sentence with coordination in Bhojpuri (lines 2–3) and Hindi (lines 4–5)

Since accuracy was very low, to improve it, we conducted three experiments solely based on Bhojpuri data to build a Bhojpuri parser. In all the three experiments, we used the UDPipe open source tool (Straka and Straková, 2017). In all the cases, we used cross-validation 90:10 average. We used UDPipe's default epoch size and learning rate, while the other hyperparameters were randomized.

However, the three experiments differ in the data size: first experiment was conducted on 1000 tokens, the second experiment was conducted on 1500 tokens, and the third experiment was conducted on 4880 tokens. The results are discussed below in the evaluation section.

Tokenization F_1	UPOS	UAS	LAS
89.15%	52.35%	56.77%	45.61%

Table 4: Accuracy of a UDPipe model trained on the Hindi UD treebank (HDTB) and applied to the first 50 Bhojpuri sentences.

6. Evaluation

The results of the three experiments with the Bhojpuri parser are shown in Table 5 and in Figure 6. In terms of labeled attachment score, the results show that the third experiment, which was trained on 4880 tokens, produced slightly better result in comparison to the previous two experiments. The third experiment also performed better in comparison to the result of the Hindi parser that was used to tag the Bhojpuri data. This result is interesting. Even though Hindi is a closely related language and its parser is trained on a large amount of data (351,704 tokens), the Hindi parser couldn't perform any better on the Bhojpuri data. This shows that the same parser should not be used on two different languages even when they are closely related. We need to develop a separate and robust parser.

	XPOS	UPOS	UAS	LAS
Experiment 1	66.67%	69.86%	39.73%	31.96%
Experiment 2	66.95%	60.17%	45.76%	35.59%
Experiment 3	77.64%	79.69%	57.49%	45.50%

Table 5: UDPipe accuracy of the conducted experiments

7. Conclusion and Future Work

This paper reports the development of the very first dependency treebank for Bhojpuri language using the annotation scheme of Universal Dependency (UD). The primary aim behind undertaking this project is to facilitate dependency treebank for Bhojpuri which is one of the low-resourced Indian languages. Currently, the Bhojpuri treebank consists of 4,881 tokens. This paper discussed the annotation guidelines used, the annotation process, and statistics of the used tags/UD relations. It also presented the linguistic analysis of the Bhojpuri treebank using examples from the language. Additionally, this paper presented a Bhojpuri parser which has been trained on UDPipe tool. The accuracy of the developed model is 57.49% UAS, 45.50% LAS, 79.69% UPOS and 77.64% XPOS.

In the near future, we plan to extend BHTB up to 5,000 sentences and develop a parallel Bhojpuri-Hindi treebank. Along with this we will improve and develop a robust Bhojpuri parser using a neural model.

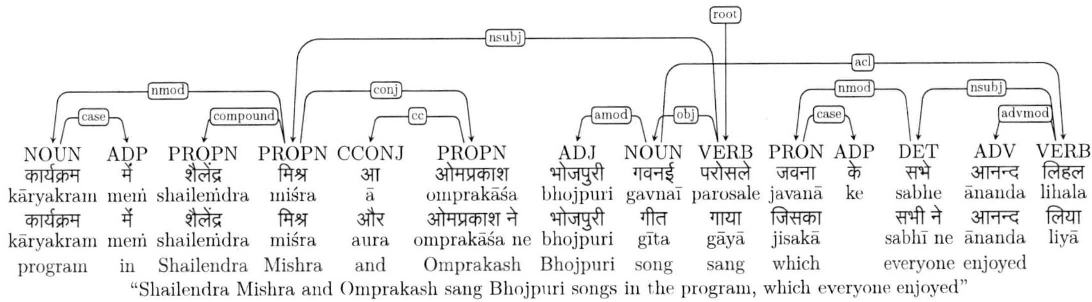

Figure 5: A parallel sentence with clauses in Bhojpuri (lines 2–3) and Hindi (lines 4–5)

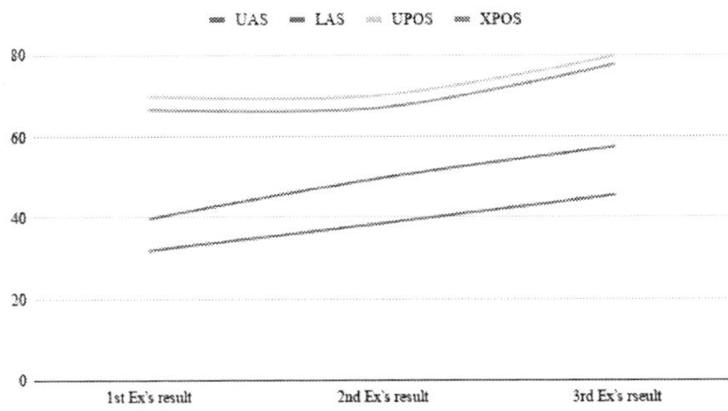

Figure 6: Learning curve of the Bhojpuri models.

8. Acknowledgements

This work has been supported by LINDAT/CLA-RIAH-CZ and Khresmoi, the grants no. LM2018101 and 7E11042 of the Ministry of Education, Youth and Sports of the Czech Republic, and FP7-ICT-2010-6-257528 of the European Union.

9. References

Begum, R., Husain, S., Dhwaj, A., Sharma, D. M., Bai, L., and Sangal, R. (2008). Dependency annotation scheme for Indian languages. In *Proceedings of the Third International Joint Conference on Natural Language Processing: Volume-II*.

Bharati, A., Chaitanya, V., and Sangal, R. (2006). *Natural Language Processing: A Paninian Perspective*. Prentice-Hall of India, New Delhi, India.

Bhat, R. A. (2017). *Exploiting linguistic knowledge to address representation and sparsity issues in dependency parsing of Indian languages*. Ph.D. thesis, PhD thesis, International Institute of Information Technology, India.

De Marneffe, M.-C. and Manning, C. D. (2008). The Stanford typed dependencies representation. In *Coling 2008: proceedings of the workshop on cross-framework and cross-domain parser evaluation*, pages 1–8. Association for Computational Linguistics.

De Marneffe, M.-C., MacCartney, B., Manning, C. D., et al. (2006). Generating typed dependency parses from phrase structure parses. In *LREC*, volume 6, pages 449–454.

De Marneffe, M.-C., Dozat, T., Silveira, N., Haverinen, K., Ginter, F., Nivre, J., and Manning, C. D. (2014). Universal Stanford dependencies: A cross-linguistic typology. In *LREC*, volume 14, pages 4585–4592.

Husain, S., Mannem, P., Ambati, B. R., and Gadde, P. (2010). The ICON-2010 tools contest on Indian language dependency parsing. *Proceedings of ICON-2010 Tools Contest on Indian Language Dependency Parsing, ICON*, 10:1–8.

Kumar, R., Lahiri, B., Alok, D., Ojha, A. K., Jain, M., Basit, A., and Dawar, Y. (2018). Automatic identification of closely-related Indian languages: Resources and experiments. In Girish Nath Jha, et al., editors, *Proceedings of the Eleventh International Conference on Language Resources and Evaluation (LREC 2018)*, Paris, France, may. European Language Resources Association (ELRA).

Ojha, A. K., Behera, P., Singh, S., and Jha, G. N. (2015). Training & evaluation of POS taggers in Indo-Aryan languages: a case of Hindi, Odia and Bhojpuri. In *the proceedings of 7th Language & Technology Conference: Human Language Technologies as a Challenge for Computer Science and Linguistics*, pages 524–529.

Ojha, A. K. (2016). Developing a machine readable multilingual dictionary for Bhojpuri-Hindi-English.

Ojha, A. K. (2019). *English-Bhojpuri SMT System: Insights from the Karaka Model*. Ph.D. thesis, Ph D thesis, Jawaharlal Nehru University, New Delhi, India.

Petrov, S., Das, D., and McDonald, R. (2012). A universal part-of-speech tagset. In *Proceedings of the Eighth International Conference on Language Resources and Evaluation (LREC'12)*, pages 2089–2096, Istanbul, Turkey, May. European Language Resources Association (ELRA).

Ravishankar, V. (2017). A Universal Dependencies treebank for Marathi. In *Proceedings of the 16th International Workshop on Treebanks and Linguistic Theories*, pages 190–200.

Singh, S. and Jha, G. N. (2015). Statistical tagger for Bhojpuri (employing support vector machine). In *2015 International Conference on Ad-*

vances in Computing, Communications and Informatics (ICACCI)*, pages 1524–1529. IEEE.

Sinha, S. and Jha, G. N. (2018). Issues in conversational Sanskrit to Bhojpuri MT. In Girish Nath Jha, et al., editors, *Proceedings of the Eleventh International Conference on Language Resources and Evaluation (LREC 2018)*, Paris, France, may. European Language Resources Association (ELRA).

Straka, M. and Straková, J. (2017). Tokenizing, POS tagging, lemmatizing and parsing UD 2.0 with UD-Pipe. In *Proceedings of the CoNLL 2017 Shared Task: Multilingual Parsing from Raw Text to Universal Dependencies*, pages 88–99.

Straka, M. and Straková, J. (2019). Universal dependencies 2.4 models for UDPipe (2019-05-31). LINDAT/CLARIN digital library at the Institute of Formal and Applied Linguistics (ÚFAL), Faculty of Mathematics and Physics, Charles University.

Verma, M. K. (2003). Bhojpuri. *The Indo-Aryan Languages*, pages 515–537.

Zeman, D., Nivre, J., Abrams, M., Aepli, N., Agić, Ž., Ahrenberg, L., Aleksandravičiūtė, G., Antonsen, L., Aplonova, K., Aranzabe, M. J., Arutie, G., Asahara, M., Ateyah, L., Attia, M., Atutxa, A., Augustinus, L., Badmaeva, E., Ballesteros, M., Banerjee, E., Bank, S., Barbu Mititelu, V., Basmov, V., Batchelor, C., Bauer, J., Bellato, S., Bengoetxea, K., Berzak, Y., Bhat, I. A., Bhat, R. A., Biagetti, E., Bick, E., Bielinskienė, A., Blokland, R., Bobicev, V., Boizou, L., Borges Völker, E., Börstell, C., Bosco, C., Bouma, G., Bowman, S., Boyd, A., Brokaitė, K., Burchardt, A., Candito, M., Caron, B., Caron, G., Cavalcanti, T., Cebiroğlu Eryiğit, G., Cecchini, F. M., Celano, G. G. A., Čéplö, S., Cetin, S., Chalub, F., Choi, J., Cho, Y., Chun, J., Cignarella, A. T., Cinková, S., Collomb, A., Çöltekin, Ç., Connor, M., Courtin, M., Davidson, E., de Marneffe, M.-C., de Paiva, V., de Souza, E., Diaz de Ilarraza, A., Dickerson, C., Dione, B., Dirix, P., Dobrovoljc, K., Dozat, T., Droganova, K., Dwivedi, P., Eckhoff, H., Eli, M., Elkahky, A., Ephrem, B., Erina, O., Erjavec, T., Etienne, A., Evelyn, W., Farkas, R., Fernandez Alcalde, H., Foster, J., Freitas, C., Fujita, K., Gajdošová, K., Galbraith, D., Garcia, M., Gärdenfors, M., Garza, S., Gerdes, K., Ginter, F., Goenaga, I., Gojenola, K., Gökırmak, M., Goldberg, Y., Gómez Guinovart, X., González Saavedra, B., Griciūtė, B., Grioni, M., Grūzītis, N., Guillaume, B., Guillot-Barbance, C., Habash, N., Hajič, J., Hajič jr., J., Hämäläinen, M., Hà Mỹ, L., Han, N.-R., Harris, K., Haug, D., Heinecke, J., Hennig, F., Hladká, B., Hlaváčová, J., Hociung, F., Hohle, P., Hwang, J., Ikeda, T., Ion, R., Irimia, E., Ishola, Q., Jelínek, T., Johannsen, A., Jørgensen, F., Juutinen, M., Kaşıkara, H., Kaasen, A., Kabaeva, N., Kahane, S., Kanayama, H., Kanerva, J., Katz, B., Kayadelen, T., Kenney, J., Kettnerová, V., Kirchner, J., Klementieva, E., Köhn, A., Kopacewicz, K., Kotsyba, N., Kovalevskaitė, J., Krek, S., Kwak, S., Laippala, V., Lambertino, L., Lam, L., Lando, T., Larasati, S. D., Lavrentiev, A., Lee, J., Lê Hồng, P., Lenci, A., Lertpradit, S., Leung, H., Li, C. Y., Li, J., Li, K., Lim, K., Liovina, M., Li, Y., Ljubešić, N., Loginova, O., Lyashevskaya, O., Lynn, T., Macketanz, V., Makazhanov, A., Mandl, M., Manning, C., Manurung, R., Mărănduc, C., Mareček, D., Marheinecke, K., Martínez Alonso, H., Martins, A., Mašek, J., Matsumoto, Y., McDonald, R., McGuinness, S., Mendonça, G., Miekka, N., Misirpashayeva, M., Missilä, A., Mititelu, C., Mitrofan, M., Miyao, Y., Montemagni, S., More, A., Moreno Romero, L., Mori, K. S., Morioka, T., Mori, S., Moro, S., Mortensen, B., Moskalevskyi, B., Muischnek, K., Munro, R., Murawaki, Y., Müürisep, K., Nainwani, P., Navarro Horñiacek, J. I., Nedoluzhko, A., Nešpore-Bērzkalne, G., Nguyễn Thị, L., Nguyễn Thị Minh, H., Nikaido, Y., Nikolaev, V., Nitisaroj, R., Nurmi, H., Ojala, S., Ojha, A. K., Olúòkun, A., Omura, M., Osenova, P., Östling, R., Øvrelid, L., Partanen, N., Pascual, E., Passarotti, M., Patejuk, A., Paulino-Passos, G., Peljak-Łapińska, A., Peng, S., Perez, C.-A., Perrier, G., Petrova, D., Petrov, S., Phelan, J., Piitulainen, J., Pirinen, T. A., Pitler, E., Plank, B., Poibeau, T., Ponomareva, L., Popel, M., Pretkalniņa, L., Prévost, S., Prokopidis, P., Przepiórkowski, A., Puolakainen, T., Pyysalo, S., Qi, P., Rääbis, A., Rademaker, A., Ramasamy, L., Rama, T., Ramisch, C., Ravishankar, V., Real, L., Reddy, S., Rehm, G., Riabov, I., Rießler, M., Rimkutė, E., Rinaldi, L., Rituma, L., Rocha, L., Romanenko, M., Rosa, R., Rovati, D., Roşca, V., Rudina, O., Rueter, J., Sadde, S., Sagot, B., Saleh, S., Salomoni, A., Samardžić, T., Samson, S., Sanguinetti, M., Särg, D., Saulīte, B., Sawanakunanon, Y., Schneider, N., Schuster, S., Seddah, D., Seeker, W., Seraji, M., Shen, M., Shimada, A., Shirasu, H., Shohibussirri, M., Sichinava, D., Silveira, A., Silveira, N., Simi, M., Simionescu, R., Simkó, K., Šimková, M., Simov, K., Smith, A., Soares-Bastos, I., Spadine, C., Stella, A., Straka, M., Strnadová, J., Suhr, A., Sulubacak, U., Suzuki, S., Szántó, Z., Taji, D., Takahashi, Y., Tamburini, F., Tanaka, T., Tellier, I., Thomas, G., Torga, L., Trosterud, T., Trukhina, A., Tsarfaty, R., Tyers, F., Uematsu, S., Urešová, Z., Uria, L., Uszkoreit, H., Utka, A., Vajjala, S., van Niekerk, D., van Noord, G., Varga, V., Villemonte de la Clergerie, E., Vincze, V., Wallin, L., Walsh, A., Wang, J. X., Washington, J. N., Wendt, M., Williams, S., Wirén, M., Wittern, C., Woldemariam, T., Wong, T.-s., Wróblewska, A., Yako, M., Yamazaki, N., Yan, C., Yasuoka, K., Yavrumyan, M. M., Yu, Z., Žabokrtský, Z., Zeldes, A., Zhang, M., and Zhu, H. (2019). Universal dependencies 2.5. LINDAT/CLARIN digital library at the Institute of Formal and Applied Linguistics (ÚFAL), Faculty of Mathematics and Physics, Charles University.

Zeman, D. (2008). Reusable tagset conversion using tagset drivers. In *LREC*, volume 2008, pages 28–30.

Proceedings of the WILDRE5– 5th Workshop on Indian Language Data: Resources and Evaluation, pages 39–44
Language Resources and Evaluation Conference (LREC 2020), Marseille, 11–16 May 2020
© European Language Resources Association (ELRA), licensed under CC-BY-NC

A Fully Expanded Dependency Treebank for Telugu

Sneha Nallani, Manish Shrivastava, Dipti Misra Sharma
Kohli Center on Intelligent Systems (KCIS),
International Institute of Information Technology, Hyderabad (IIIT-H)
Gachibowli, Hyderabad, Telangana-500032, India
sneha.nallani@research.iiit.ac.in, {m.shrivastava, dipti}@iiit.ac.in

Abstract

Treebanks are an essential resource for syntactic parsing. The available Paninian dependency treebank(s) for Telugu is annotated only with inter-chunk dependency relations and not all words of a sentence are part of the parse tree. In this paper, we automatically annotate the intra-chunk dependencies in the treebank using a Shift-Reduce parser based on Context Free Grammar rules for Telugu chunks. We also propose a few additional intra-chunk dependency relations for Telugu apart from the ones used in Hindi treebank. Annotating intra-chunk dependencies finally provides a complete parse tree for every sentence in the treebank. Having a fully expanded treebank is crucial for developing end to end parsers which produce complete trees. We present a fully expanded dependency treebank for Telugu consisting of 3220 sentences. In this paper, we also convert the treebank annotated with Anncorra part-of-speech tagset to the latest BIS tagset. The BIS tagset is a hierarchical tagset adopted as a unified part-of-speech standard across all Indian Languages. The final treebank is made publicly available.

Keywords: Dependency Treebank, Intra-chunk dependencies, Low resource Language, Telugu

1. Introduction

Treebanks play a crucial role in developing parsers as well as investigating other linguistic phenomena. Which is why there has been a targeted effort to create treebanks in several languages. Some such notable efforts include the Penn treebank (Marcus et al., 1993), the Prague Dependency treebank (Hajičová, 1998). A treebank is annotated with a grammar. The grammars used for annotating treebanks can be broadly categorized into two types, Context Free Grammars and dependency grammars. A Context Free Grammar consists of a set of rules that determine how the words and symbols of a language can be grouped together and a lexicon consisting of words and symbols. Dependency grammars on the other hand model the syntactic relationship between the words of a sentence directly using head-dependent relations. Dependency grammars are useful in modeling free word order languages. Indian languages are primarily free word order languages. There are few different dependency formalisms that have been developed for different languages. In recent years, Universal dependencies(Nivre et al., 2016) have been developed to arrive at a common dependency formalism for all languages. Paninian dependency grammar(Bharati et al., 1995) is specifically developed for Indian languages which are morphologically rich and free word order languages. Case markers and postpositions play crucial roles in these languages and word order is considered only at a surface level when required.

Most Indian languages are also low resource languages. ICON-2009 and 2010 tools contests made available the initial dependency treebanks for Hindi, Telugu and Bangla. These treebanks are small in size and are annotated using the Paninian dependency grammar. Further efforts are being taken to build dependency annotated treebanks for Indian languages. Hindi and Urdu multi-layered and multi-representational (Bhat et al., 2009) treebanks have been developed. Treebanks are also being developed for Bengali, Kannada, Hindi, Malayalam and Marathi as part of the Indian Language Treebanking project. These treebanks are annotated in Shakti Standard Format(SSF)(Bharati et al., 2007). Each sentence is annotated at word level with part of speech tags, at morphological level with root, gender, number, person, TAM, vibhakti and case features and the dependency relations are annotated at a chunk level. The dependency relations within a chunk are left unannotated. Intra-chunk dependency annotation has been done on Hindi(Kosaraju et al., 2012) and Urdu(Bhat, 2017) treebanks previously. Annotating intra-chunk dependencies leads to a complete parse tree for every sentence in the treebank. Having completely annotated parse trees is essential for building robust end to end dependency parsers or making the treebanks available in CoNLL (Buchholz and Marsi, 2006) format and thereby making use of readily available parsers. In this paper, we extend one of those approaches for the Telugu treebank to annotate intra-chunk dependency relations. Telugu is a highly inflected morphologically rich language and has a few constructions like classifiers etc that do not occur in Hindi which makes the expansion task challenging. The fully expanded Telugu treebank is made publicly available [1].

The part-of-speech and chunk annotation of the Telugu treebank is done following the Anncorra (Bharati et al., 2009b) tagset developed for Indian languages. In the recent years, there has been a co-ordinated effort to develop a Unified Parts-of-Speech (POS) Standard that can be adopted across all Indian Languages. This tagset is commonly referred to as the BIS [2] (Bureau of Indian standards) tagset. All the latest annotation of part of speech tagging of Indian languages is done using the BIS tagset. In this paper, we convert the existing Telugu treebank from Anncorra to BIS standard. BIS tagset is a fine grained hierarchical tagset

---

[1] https://github.com/ltrc/telugu_treebank

[2] The BIS tagset is made available at http://tdil-dc.in/tdildcMain/articles/134692Draft%20POS%20Tag%20standard.pdf

and many Anncorra tags diverge into finer grained BIS categories. This makes the conversion task challenging.

The rest of the paper is organised as follows. In section 2, we describe the Telugu Dependency Treebank, section 3 describes the part of speech conversion from Anncorra to BIS standard, section 4 describes the intra-chunk dependency relations annotation for the Telugu and we conclude the paper in section 5.

2. Telugu Treebank

An initial Telugu treebank consisting of around 1600 sentences is made available in ICON 2009 tools contest. This treebank is combined with HCU Telugu treebank containing approximately 2000 sentences similarly annotated and another 200 sentences annotated at IIIT Hyderabad. We clean up the treebank by removing sentences with wrong format or incomplete parse trees etc. The final treebank consists of 3220 sentences. Details about the treebank are listed in Table 1.

No. of sentences	3222
Avg. sent length	5.5 words
Avg. no of chunks in sent	4.2
Avg. length of a chunk	1.3 words

Table 1: Telugu treebank stats

The treebank is annotated using Paninian dependency grammar(Bharati et al., 1995). The paninian dependency relations are created around the notion of karakas, various participants in an action. These dependency relations are syntacto-semantic in nature. There are 40 different dependency labels specified in the panianian dependency grammar. These relations are hierarchical and certain relations can be under-specified in cases where a finer analysis is not required or when in certain cases the decision making is more difficult for the annotators(Bharati et al., 2009b). Begum et al. (2008) describe the guidelines for annotating dependency relations for Indian languages using paninian dependencies. The treebank is annotated with part-of-speech tags and morphological information like root, gender, number, person, TAM, vibhakti or case markers etc at word level. The dependency relations are annotated at chunk level. The treebank is made available in SSF format(Bharati et al., 2007). An example is shown in Figure 1. The dependency tree for the sentence is shown in Figure 2.

In the example sentence, the intra-chunk dependencies, i.e dependency labels for *cAlA (many)* and *I (this)* are not annotated. Only the chunk heads, *xeSAllo (countries-in)* and *parisWiwi (situation)* are annotated as the children of *lexu (is-not-there)*.

The dependency treebanks are manually annotated and it is a time consuming process. In AnnCorra formalism for Indian languages, a chunk is defined as a minimal, non recursive phrase consisting of correlated, inseparable words or entities (Bharati et al., 2009a). Since the dependencies within a chunk can be easily and accurately identified based on a few rules specific to a language, these dependencies have not been annotated in the initial phase. But

```
<Sentence id='10'>
1    ((    NP   <fs af='xeSaM,n,,pl,,,lo,lo' head="xeSAllo" drel='k7p:VGF' name='NP'>
1.1  cAlA QT_QTF  <fs af='cAlA,avy,,,,,0,0_avy'>
1.2  xeSAllo   N_NN     <fs af='xeSaM,n,,pl,,,lo,lo' name="xeSAllo">
     ))
2    ((    NP   <fs af='parisWiwi,n,,sg,,d,0,0' head="parisWiwi" drel='k1:VGF' name='NP2'>
2.1  I     DM_DMD <fs af='I,avy,,,,,,' poslcat="NM">
2.2  parisWiwi N_NN     <fs af='parisWiwi,n,,sg,,d,0,0' name="parisWiwi">
     ))
3    ((    VGF <fs af='gala,v,fn,sg,3,,a,a' head="lexu" name='VGF'>
3.1  lexu V_VM     <fs af='gala,v,fn,sg,3,,a,a' name="lexu">
3.2  .     RD_PUNC     <fs af='.,punc,,,,,,' poslcat="NM">
     ))
</Sentence>
```

Figure 1: Inter-chunk dependency annotation in SSF format

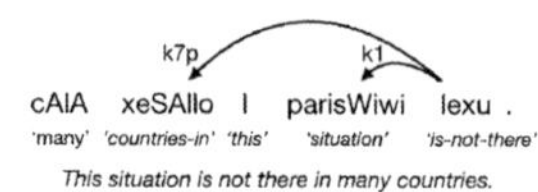

Figure 2: Inter-chunk dependency tree.

inter-chunk annotation alone does not provide a fully constructed parse tree for the sentence. Hence it is important to determine and annotate intra-chunk relations accurately. In this paper, we expand the Telugu treebank by annotating the intra-chunk dependency relations.

3. Part-of-Speech Conversion

The newly annotated 200 sentences in the treebank are annotated with the BIS tagset while the rest are annotated using Anncorra tagset. We convert the sentences with Anncorra POS tags to BIS tags so that the treebank is uniformly annotated and adheres to the latest standards.

Anncorra tagset Bharati et al. (2009a) propose the POS standard for annotating Indian Languages. This standard has been developed as part of the guidelines for annotating corpora in Indian Languages for the Indian Language Machine Translation (ILMT) project and is commonly referred to as Anncorra POS tagset. The tagset consists of a total of 26 tags.

BIS tagset The BIS (Bureau of Indian standards) tagset is a unified POS Standard in Indian Languages developed to standardize the POS tagging of all the Indian Languages. This tagset is hierarchical and at the top most level consists of 11 POS categories. Most of these categories are further divided into several fine-grained POS tags. The annotators can choose the level of coarseness required. They can use the highest level tags for a coarse grained tagset or go deeper down the hierarchy for more fine-grained tags. The fine-grained tags automatically contain the information of the parent tags. For example, the tag V_VM_VF specifies that the word is a verb (V), a main verb(V_VM) and a finite main verb (V_VM_VF).

3.1. Converting Anncorra to BIS

For most tags present in the the Anncorra tagset, there is a direct one on one mapping to a BIS tag. However, there are a few tags in Anncorra which diverge in to many fine-grained BIS categories. Those tags are shown in Table 2. It should be noted that one to many mapping exists only with fine grained tags. There is still a one to one mapping between the Anncorra tag and the corresponding parent BIS tag in all cases except question words.

Anncorra POS tag	BIS POS tag
PRP (Pronoun)	PR_PRP, PR_PRF, PR_PRL, PR_PRC, PR_PRQ
DEM (Demonstrative)	DM_DMD, DM_DMR, DM_DMQ
VM (Main verb)	V_VM_VF, V_VM_VNF, V_VM_VINF, V_VM_VNG, N_NNV
CC (Conjunct)	CC_CCD, CC_CCS
WQ (Question word)	DM_DMQ, PR_PRQ
SYM (Symbol)	RD_SYM, RD_PUNC
RDP (Reduplicative)	-
*C (Compound)	-

Table 2: Fine grained BIS tags corresponding to Anncorra tags.

During conversion, we aim to annotate with the most fine grained BIS tag. When the fine-grained tag cannot be determined we go the parent tag. We use a tagset converter that maps various tags in Anncorra schema to the tags in BIS schema. In case of tags having multiple possibilities, a list based approach is used. Most Anncorra tags diverging into fine grained BIS tags are for function words which are limited in number. Separate lists consisting of words belonging to fine grained BIS categories are created. A word is annotated with fine grained BIS tag if it is present in the corresponding tag word list, otherwise it is annotated with the parent tag.

Pronouns One of the main distinctions between the two tagsets is in the annotation of pronouns. In Anncorra, all pronouns are annotated with a single tag, PRP. BIS schema contains separate tags for annotating personal (PR_PRP) pronouns, reflexive (PR_PRF), relative (PR_PRL), reciprocal (PR_PRC) pronouns and question words (PR_PRQ). Pronouns in a language are generally limited in number. In Telugu however, pronouns can be inflected with case markers and there can be a huge number of them. When a pronoun is not found in any word list it is annotated with the parent tag PR.

Demonstratives In Anncorra, there is a single tag for annotating demonstratives where as BIS tagset distinguishes between diectic, relative and question-word demonstratives. Demonstratives are limited in number and the same list based approach used for pronouns is applied here.

Symbols Symbols are separated into symbols and punctuations.

Question words They are separated into pronoun question words and demonstrative question words in BIS tagset. Demonstrative question words are always followed by a noun. While resolving question words (WQ), if the word

is followed by a noun it is marked as DM_DMQ, else it is marked as PR_PRQ.

Verbs Another distinction between the two tagsets lies in the annotation of verb finiteness. In Anncorra, it is annotated only at chunk level. In BIS schema, the finiteness can be annotated at word level. While resolving Verbs (V_VM), we look at the verb chunk. There is a one to one mapping between Anncorra chunk types and the fine-grained BIS verb categories.

Compounds and reduplicatives In Anncorra schema, there are separate tags for identifying reduplicatives(RDP) and part of compounds(*C). For example a noun compound consisting of two words is tagged as NNC and NN. Examples of reduplicative and noun compound constructions in Telugu are shown below.

Anncorra: *maMci (good)_JJ maMci (good)_RDP cIralu (sarees)_NN*
BIS: *maMci_JJ maMci_JJ cIralu_N_NN*

Anncorra: *boVppAyi (papaya)_NNC kAya (fruit)_NN*
BIS: *boVppAyi_N_NN kAya_N_NN*

These two tags are done away with in the BIS schema. Reduplicatives (RDP) are marked with POS tag of the word preceding it and Compounds(*C) are marked with the POS tag of the word following it.

4. Annotating Intra-chunk Dependencies

The intra-chunk annotation in SSF format for the sentence in Figure 1 is shown in Figure 4 and the fully expanded dependency tree is shown in Figure 3.

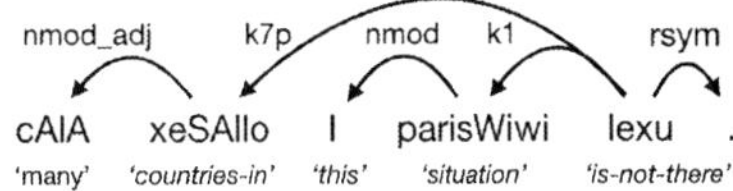

Figure 3: Intra-chunk dependency tree.

It can be seen that, in this case, unlike in Figure 2, *cAIA (many)* is attached to its chunk head, *xeSAllo (countries-in)* and *I (this)* is attached its chunk head *parisWiwi (situation)*. The parse tree for the sentence is now complete. Complete parse trees are useful for creating end to end parsers which do not require intermediate pipeline tools like POS taggers, morphological analyzers and shallow parsers. This is a huge advantage, especially for low resource languages like Telugu.

Kosaraju et al. (2012) first proposed the guidelines for annotating intra-chunk dependency relations in SSF format for Hindi. They propose a total of 12 intra-chunk dependency labels mentioned in Table 2. *lwg_* refers to *local word group* and *pof_* refers to *part of*.

They also propose two approaches, one rule based and another statistical for automatically annotating intra-chunk dependencies in Hindi. In the rule based approach several rules are created constrained upon the POS, chunk name or type and the position of the chunk head with respect to the child node. The intra-chunk dependencies are

```
<Sentence id="10">
1   cAIA      QT_QTF <fs af='cAIA,avy,,,,,0,0_avy' drel='nmod__adj:xeSAllo' name='cAIA' chunkType='child:NP'>
2   xeSAllo N_NN   <fs af='xeSaM,n,,pl,,,lo,lo' drel='k7p:lexu' vpos='vib2' name='xeSAllo' chunkId='NP' chunkType='head:NP'>
3   I   DM_DMD     <fs poslcat='NM' drel='nmod:parisWiwi' af='I,avy,,,,,,' name='I' chunkType='child:NP2'>
4   parisWiwi  N_NN   <fs af='parisWiwi,n,,sg,,d,0,0' drel='k1:lexu' name='parisWiwi' chunkId='NP2' chunkType='head:NP2'>
5   lexu V_VM   <fs af='gala,v,fn,sg,3,,a,a' name='lexu' chunkId='VGF' chunkType='head:VGF'>
6   .   RD_PUNC   <fs poslcat='NM' drel='rsym:lexu' af='.,punc,,,,,' name='.' chunkType='child:VGF'>
</Sentence>
```

Figure 4: Intra-chunk dependency annotation in SSF format.

marked based on these rules. In the statistical approach Malt Parser(Nivre et al., 2006) is used to identify the intra-chunk dependencies. A model is trained on a few manually annotated chunks with Malt parser and the same model is used to predict the intra-chunk dependencies for the rest of the treebank.

nmod__adj	adjectives modifying nouns or pronouns
lwg__psp	post-positions
lwg__neg	negation
lwg__vaux	verb auxiliaries
lwg__rp	particles
lwg__uh	interjection
lwg__cont	continuation
pof__redup	reduplication
pof__cn	compound nouns
pof__cv	compound verbs
jjmod__intf	adjectival intensifier
rsym	symbols

Table 3: Intra-chunk dependencies proposed for Hindi

Bhat (2017) propose a different approach for annotating intra-chunk dependencies for Hindi and Urdu by combining both rule based and statistical approaches. Instead of a completely rule based system, they create a Context Free Grammar(CFG) for identifying intra-chunk dependencies. The dependencies within a chunk are annotated based on the CFG using a shift reduce parser.

4.1. Intra-chunk dependency annotation for Telugu treebank

In addition to the twelve dependency labels proposed for Hindi, we also introduce a few more labels, **nmod**, **nmod__wq**, **adv** and **intf** for annotating intra-chunk dependencies for Telugu treebank. *nmod* and *adv* are already present in the inter-chunk dependency labels (Bharati et al., 2009b).

nmod This dependency relation is used when demonstratives, proper nouns, pronouns and quantifiers modify a noun or pronoun.

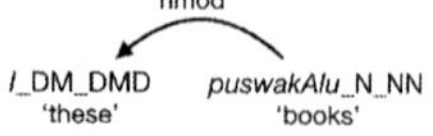

intf Intensifiers (RP_INTF) can modify both adjectives and adverbs. So we replace the *jjmod__intf* with *intf* and use the same dependency label when an intensifier modifies an adverb or adjective.

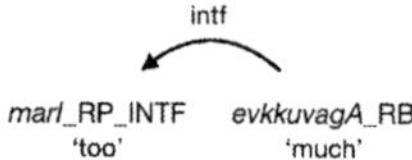

nmod__wq This dependency relation is used when question words modify nouns inside a chunk.

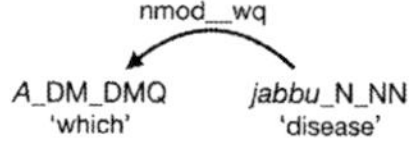

adv This dependency relation is used when adverbs modify a verb inside a chunk.

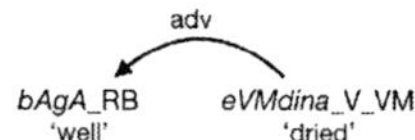

pof__cv Compound verbs are combined together in Telugu. So this dependency relation is not seen in Telugu. An example of compound verb is *kOsEswAnu*. It is a compound of *kOsi* and *vEs-wAnu*. In cases like *ceyyAlsi vaccindi*, *vaccindi* is annotated as an auxiliary verb.

lwg__rp This dependency label is used to annotate particles like *gAru*, *kUdA* etc. It is also used for classifiers. Telugu contains classifiers and a commonly used classifier is *maMxi*. It specifies that the noun following *maMxi* is human. Sometimes the following noun can be dropped and in those cases *maMxi* is treated as a noun. Classifiers are cat-

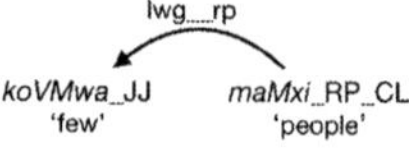

egorized under particles. So, *maMxi* is marked as a child of *koVMwa* using label *lwg__rp* in the above example.

lwg__psp In Telugu most post-positions occur as inflections of content words. But few of them also occur separately. The ones occurring separately are marked as *lwg_psp*. Sometimes, spatio-temporal nouns (N_NST) also act as post-positions when occurring alongside nouns. In these cases, they are annotated as *lwg_psp*.

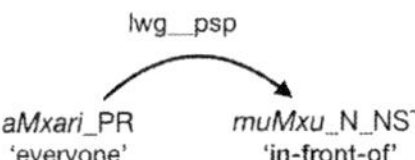

In this paper, we follow the approach proposed by Bhat (2017) that makes use of a Context Free Grammar (CFG) and a shift-reduce parser for automatically annotating intra-chunk dependencies. We use the treebank expander code made available by Bhat (2017) [3] and write the Context Free Grammar for Telugu. The Context Free Grammar is generated using the POS tags and creates a mapping between head and child POS tags and dependency labels.

The intra-chunk annotation is done using a shift-reduce parser which internally uses the Arc-Standard(Nivre, 2004) transition system. The parser predicts a sequence of transitions starting from an initial configuration to a terminal configuration, and annotate the chunk dependencies in the process. A configuration consists of a stack, a buffer, and a set of dependency arcs. In the initial configuration, the stack is empty, buffer contains all the words in the chunk and intra-chunk dependencies are empty. In the terminal configuration, buffer is empty and stack contains only one element, the chunk head, and the chunk sub-tree is given by the set of dependency arcs. The next transition is predicted based on the Context Free Grammar and the current configuration.

4.1.1. Results

We evaluate intra-chunk dependency relations annotated by the parser for 106 sentences. The test set evaluation results are shown in Table 4.

Test sentences	LAS	UAS
106	93.7	95.8

Table 4: Intra-chunk dependency annotation accuracies.

Almost all of the wrongly annotated chunks are because of POS errors or chunk boundary errors. Since the Context Free Grammar rules are written using POS tags, errors in annotation of POS tags automatically lead to errors in intra-chunk dependency annotation. The dependency relations are annotated within the chunk boundaries. So any errors in the chunk boundary identification also lead to errors in intra-chunk dependency annotation.

Telugu is an agglutinative language and the chunk size rarely exceeds three words. The CFG grammar based approach works accurately provided there are no errors in POS or chunk annotation.

[3] https://github.com/ltrc/
Shift-Reduce-Chunk-Expander

5. Conclusion

In this paper, we automatically annotate the Telugu dependency treebank with intra-chunk dependency relations thus finally providing complete parse trees for every sentence in the treebank. We also convert the Telugu treebank from AnnCorra part-of-speech tagset to the latest BIS tagset. We make the fully expanded Telugu treebank publicly available to facilitate further research.

6. Acknowledgements

We would like to thank Himanshu Sharma for making the Hindi tagset converter code available and Parameshwari Krishnamurthy and Pruthwik Mishra for providing relevant input. We also thank all the reviewers for their insightful comments.

7. Bibliographical References

Begum, R., Husain, S., Dhwaj, A., Sharma, D. M., Bai, L., and Sangal, R. (2008). Dependency annotation scheme for indian languages. In *Proceedings of the Third International Joint Conference on Natural Language Processing: Volume-II*.

Bharati, A., Chaitanya, V., Sangal, R., and Ramakrishnamacharyulu, K. (1995). *Natural language processing: a Paninian perspective*. Prentice-Hall of India New Delhi.

Bharati, A., Sangal, R., and Sharma, D. M. (2007). Ssf: Shakti standard format guide. *Language Technologies Research Centre, International Institute of Information Technology, Hyderabad, India*, pages 1–25.

Bharati, A., Sharma, D. M., Bai, L., and Sangal, R. (2009a). Anncorra : Annotating corpora guidelines for pos and chunk annotation for indian languages. *LTRC, IIIT Hyderabad*.

Bharati, A., Sharma, D. M., Husain, S., Bai, L., Begam, R., and Sangal, R. (2009b). Anncorra: Treebanks for indian languages, guidelines for annotating hindi treebank. *LTRC, IIIT Hyderabad*.

Bhat, R. A. (2017). *Exploiting linguistic knowledge to address representation and sparsity issues in dependency parsing of indian languages*. Phd thesis, IIIT Hyderabad.

Bhatt, R., Narasimhan, B., Palmer, M., Rambow, O., Sharma, D., and Xia, F. (2009). A multi-representational and multi-layered treebank for Hindi/Urdu. In *Proceedings of the Third Linguistic Annotation Workshop (LAW III)*, pages 186–189, Suntec, Singapore, August. Association for Computational Linguistics.

Buchholz, S. and Marsi, E. (2006). CoNLL-x shared task on multilingual dependency parsing. In *Proceedings of the Tenth Conference on Computational Natural Language Learning (CoNLL-X)*, pages 149–164, New York City, June. Association for Computational Linguistics.

Hajičová, E. (1998). Prague dependency treebank: From analytic to tectogrammatical annotations. *Proceedings of 2nd TST, Brno, Springer-Verlag Berlin Heidelberg New York*, pages 45–50.

Kosaraju, P., Ambati, B. R., Husain, S., Sharma, D. M., and Sangal, R. (2012). Intra-chunk dependency annotation : Expanding Hindi inter-chunk annotated treebank.

In *Proceedings of the Sixth Linguistic Annotation Workshop*, pages 49–56, Jeju, Republic of Korea, July. Association for Computational Linguistics.

Marcus, M. P., Santorini, B., and Marcinkiewicz, M. A. (1993). Building a large annotated corpus of English: The Penn Treebank. *Computational Linguistics*, 19(2):313–330.

Nivre, J., Hall, J., and Nilsson, J. (2006). MaltParser: A data-driven parser-generator for dependency parsing. In *Proceedings of the Fifth International Conference on Language Resources and Evaluation (LREC'06)*, Genoa, Italy, May. European Language Resources Association (ELRA).

Nivre, J., de Marneffe, M.-C., Ginter, F., Goldberg, Y., Hajič, J., Manning, C. D., McDonald, R., Petrov, S., Pyysalo, S., Silveira, N., Tsarfaty, R., and Zeman, D. (2016). Universal dependencies v1: A multilingual treebank collection. In *Proceedings of the Tenth International Conference on Language Resources and Evaluation (LREC'16)*, pages 1659–1666, Portorož, Slovenia, May. European Language Resources Association (ELRA).

Nivre, J. (2004). Incrementality in deterministic dependency parsing. In *Proceedings of the Workshop on Incremental Parsing: Bringing Engineering and Cognition Together*, pages 50–57, Barcelona, Spain, July. Association for Computational Linguistics.

Proceedings of the WILDRE5– 5th Workshop on Indian Language Data: Resources and Evaluation, pages 45–50
Language Resources and Evaluation Conference (LREC 2020), Marseille, 11–16 May 2020

Determination of Idiomatic Sentences in Paragraphs Using Statement Classification and Generalization of Grammar Rules

Naziya Mahamdul Shaikh

Government College of Arts, Science and Commerce
Quepem-Goa, India
naziya1019@gmail.com

Abstract

The translation systems are often not able to determine the presence of an idiom in a given paragraph. Due to this many systems tend to return the word-for-word translation of such statements leading to loss in the flavor of the idioms in the paragraph. This paper suggests a novel approach to efficiently determine probability of any statement in a given English paragraph to be an idiom. This approach combines the rule-based generalization of idioms in English language and classification of statements based on the context to determine the idioms in the sentence. The context based classification method can be used further for determination of idioms in regional Indian languages such as Marathi, Konkani and Hindi as the difference in the semantic context of the proverb as compared to the context in a paragraph is also evident in these languages.

Keywords: idioms, rule-based generalization, classification

1. Introduction

Most translation systems are able to reasonably translate one language to another. But many fail when it comes to translation of the idioms in a language. Idioms are multi word expressions and the correct translation of such expression requires usage of completely different semantic context in a different language which is difficult to achieve using direct translation method. For translating idioms, system must first determine that the given sentence in a paragraph is an idiom and once identified, search for it from a large corpus storing the proverbs which requires a lot of processing. Therefore most systems prefer to treat idioms like any other general language sentence and provide literal meaning instead of a semantically equivalent statement in target language that would actually provide the flavor of the idiom to the given paragraph. Certain other systems would simply carry out search through a large corpus of stored idioms which is also very time-consuming. A new method is needed towards finding idioms in a paragraph efficiently. Further after determining idioms, processing is required to search for translation of such idioms with the correct words denoting semantic translation of the same in the target language. A new method of storage that can reduce the amount of time required for the search would greatly enhance the translation process of the idiomatic sentences.

2. Related Work

Various types of studies have been done on the structural compositions of the proverbs in different languages. One of the theories treats the proverbs as a species of metaphors (Coinnigh, 2013). Other anthropological, folkloric, and performance-based studies were carried out over the use of various proverbs in different cultural settings (Bradbury, 2002).

For finding the proverb in the given paragraph, certain methods have been used in the recent years. In one method, each statement in the paragraph is taken, all the inflections in the statement are removed and the statement is compared with the entire exhaustive list of stored proverbs for a match (Pisharoty et al., 2012). But this method does not provide an optimized approach. As the

size of the input paragraph gets larger, the processing required for this method also increases greatly. In another study, idioms are treated as any other statement to be parsed into parts of speech tags until a pattern is recognized based on the threshold. Based on the activation achieved using grammar based parsing, a new additional process is added for the idioms (Stock, 1989). One of the methods uses a proverb translation system in which source language text are searched and their equivalents in target language are produced using single word information.(Brahmaleen et al., 2010) In this method, input is split into single word units and saved in one dimensional array. Proverb is also split into single word units and saved as a row in two dimensional array. The two arrays are compared to determine whether the statement is a proverb. A linguistic characteristic called verb-object collocations used to determine the asymmetry in the semantics between a verb in the statement and the corresponding object in the same statement is used in the determination of the idiomatic statements (Tapanainen et al., 1998). Yet another method used for determination of proverbs (Coinnigh, 2013) focuses on the metaphors present in the statements likely to be a proverb. This study analyzed the frequency, nature and form of metaphor in Irish-language proverbs. This study claimed metaphors could be secondary proverbial markers. For the translation of the proverbs, current method either uses direct storage of list of proverbs along with their translation to be searched with sequential accesses (Pisharoty et al., 2012) or uses complete ignorance of the proverb and does word-for-word literal translation for the proverb. Yet another method (Goyal and Sharma, 2011) uses a simple relational data approach after extracting the static part of the Hindi language proverb from the sentence, handled by using regular expression. The commonalities in the methods used in translation of proverb in Indian languages like Marathi were also studied and the methods used for translation were generalized into common strategies (Dash, 2016).

3. Proposed Work

This paper presents an idea to determine the idioms in a given paragraph using certain generalized rules related to the grammar which are common for most of the idiom statements in that language. The results of this method can then be combined with classification based method to improve the probability of a given statement being an idiom.

3.1 Determination of Statement as an Idiom

3.1.1 Classification Method

The classification method includes classifying a given statement into a general category. Idioms in a paragraph generally tend to belong to a different context as compared to the actual paragraph content. Using this fact, the category of the entire paragraph is compared with the category of the statement. The difference between the two categories is measured. The higher the difference more is the probability of any given sentence being an idiom. The same concept can be enhanced and further developed cross linguistically for regional languages like Hindi, Marathi and Konkani because the proverbs in most languages generally consist of a completely different semantic context as compared to the context of the remaining paragraph.

3.1.2 Generalized Rules Method

Certain rules of the English language usually apply for most of the idioms in a paragraph. After observation of several proverbs in the language, we can assume in general, that the rules include facts like - most of the idioms tend to be in present tense, idioms are usually said in active voices, an idiom statement usually does not contain a personal pronoun unless the pronoun is placed at start of the statement along with a subject pronoun in the same sentence. For example, consider a statement like: "He will fail as he has not planned properly" versus an idiomatic statement like "he who is failing to plan, is planning to fail". In the first statement, personal pronoun 'He' is not followed by a subject pronoun. Whereas in second statement, a subject pronoun 'who' follows.

Also presence of a clause is very common whenever a sentence includes an idiom. Consider for example the phrases in the paragraph like: "But you know what they say, don't judge a book by its cover" or "It has been rightly said that whenever there is a will, there will always be a way". In such cases, there is high amount of usage of certain limited set of words such as 'realized', 'told', 'said', 'knew', 'say' and few more. All these rules can be generalized and used as criterias to indicate the presence of an idiom in a sentence. An algorithm can be written to check for these rules in each statement and accordingly assign weightage to each criteria for that statement. The higher the scoring for each criteria, more is the probability of the statement being an idiom.

3.2 Development of POS Tags Based Data Structure for Better Access of the Proverb Translations

To provide the translation of proverbs, we need to store the proverbs and their corresponding semantically translated meaning in target languages. But due to the large number of idioms, which are required to be stored, a direct storage can cause processing issues during search operations. Therefore instead we can use a different approach for storage of these proverbs in the data structure. Ontology can be prepared which contains major adjectives and nouns in the idioms as the beginning of the access search. As the nouns and adjectives are not very common throughout the idioms, the search list can be easily filtered and the amount of search comparisons required can be lowered. When a proverb is identified in a paragraph, the proverb statement will be POS tagged and various nouns and adjectives in the proverb would be identified. Based on the nouns and adjectives in the proverb, ontology prepared as mentioned before can be searched to find the proverb and then display the corresponding semantic translation meaning.

4. Implementation

4.1.1 Classification Method

For implementation of the classification method, we find the categories of the sentence and the rest of the paragraph without that sentence. In this implementation, Application Programming Interface (API) provided by IBM Watson has been used for testing the categories. The model was not trained for any specific requirement, only the general version was used for this implementation. The general version of this API provided classification into already specified sets of categories by IBM Watson including 'style and fashion', 'law and politics', 'science', 'spirituality', 'parenting', etc. Member sets were created with various categories available in the classifier in such a way that categories that are semantically closer in context are placed into same member set. Each member set was arranged according to the similarities between the categories within it in order to determine the proximity of the categories for member sets. Based on these member sets, the difference between the categories of the given statement and the categories of the paragraphs excluding that given statement was determined. In this implementation, for simplicity, only the following grading of the category classes has been considered based on the difference determination using member sets:

Completely not matching - 4.5
Matching to some extent - 3.5
Matching well - 2
Complete match - 1.5

The following paragraph is used as sample to demonstrate the method for finding the idioms. Similarly other paragraphs were checked using the same method and the similar grading was obtained for those other paragraphs.

Paragraph:
"There is this boy in my neighborhood. He is Very strangely dressed and remains quite aloof. He has tattoos all over his body. But you know what they say, don't judge a book by its cover. So I went ahead and tried to converse with this boy. And I was right, this boy was indeed had a very interesting nature. He was just a teenager in his growing phase. That is when I realized to understand others we need to put ourselves in other people's shoes."

The results found after analyzing the given paragraph using the classifier are as shown in the table below. The table shows the category of the given statement, the category of the entire paragraph excluding the given statement and the score which is calculated using the grading based on the difference of the categories of the sentence and the remaining paragraph.

Sentence	Sentence Category	Paragraph Category	Score
There is this boy in my neighborhood.	(real estate / low income housing)-0.77 (/ home and garden / gardening and landscaping / yard and patio)- 0.25 (/ food and drink / food and grocery retailers / bakeries)-0.16	(/ style and fashion / footwear / shoes)-0.95 (/ style and fashion / body art)-0.44	3.5
He is very strangely dressed and remains quite aloof.	(/ law, govt and politics / politics)-0.43 (/ pets / cats)-0.36 (/ business and industrial / company / merger and acquisition)-0.22	(/ style and fashion / footwear / shoes)-0.95 (/ style and fashion / body art)-0.42	3.5
He has tattoos all over his body.	(/ style and fashion / beauty / tattoos)-1.00 (/ style and fashion / body art / hobbies and interests)	(/ style and fashion / footwear / shoes)	1.5
But you know what they say, don't judge a book by its cover.	(/ art and entertainment / books and literature)-0.98 (/ law, govt and politics / government / courts and judiciary)-0.05 (/ business and industrial / company / bankruptcy)-0.03	(/ style and fashion / footwear / shoes)-0.96 / style and fashion / body art 0.42	3.5
So I went ahead and tried to converse with this boy.	(/ style and fashion / footwear / sneakers)-1.00 (/ style and fashion / footwear / shoes)-0.02 (/ shopping / retail / outlet stores)	(/ style and fashion / footwear / shoes)- 0.96 (/ style and fashion / body art)-0.42	1.5
And I was right, this boy indeed had a very interesting nature.	(/ science)-0.54 (/ law, govt and politics / politics)-0.48 (/ religion and spirituality)-0.48	(/ style and fashion / footwear / shoes)- 0.96 (/ style and fashion / body art)-0.42	3.5
He was just a teenager in his growing phase.	(/ family and parenting / parenting teens)-0.96 (/ family and parenting / children)-0.10 (/ family and parenting)-0.06	(/ style and fashion / footwear / shoes)-0.96 (/ style and fashion / body art)-0.42	4.5
That is when I realized to understand others we need to put ourselves in other people's shoes.	(/ style and fashion / footwear / shoes)-1.00 (/ style and fashion / footwear / sneakers / style and fashion / footwear)	(/ style and fashion / footwear / shoes)-0.96 (/ style and fashion / body art)-0.42	1.5

Table 1: Analysis of the paragraph using the classifier

4.1.2 Generalized Rules Method

In the implementation of this method, we first generate tense of the sentence using Stanford POS Tagger (Toutanova and Manning, 2000) which provides the parts of speech tags for each word in the sentence. If the tense is any form of present tense, we assign a score based on this criterion. In this implementation, we have assigned a comparative score of 2.5 for the statement to be in present tense as this rule applies for most of the English proverbs. We further evaluate the statement to check whether the statement contains a clause and a score is assigned based on this criterion. If there are words like realized, told, etc. present along with the clause, then some more points are given to the criterion as the clauses containing these words are very common in the idiomatic statements in the paragraphs. This is followed by determination of Active/Passive voice of the sentence using Dependencies of the sentence provided by Stanford Core NLP package (Toutanova et al., 2003). After this, using the POS tags of the sentence generated before, a personal pronoun (such as he/she) is searched in the sentence. If a personal pronoun is found, we further search for a subject pronoun (such as who) in the same sentence. We also check the position of the personal pronoun in the sentence. After observation of different pronouns in the language, the rule has been generalized stating that if only a personal pronoun is present, sentence is usually not found to be an idiom. Therefore we decrement the score in this case. Whereas if personal pronoun is present and also subject pronoun is present and the personal pronoun is placed before the subject pronoun, then the statement may be an idiom. So we add to the score based on this criterion.

A general algorithm has been written using Java packages to check for the tense, clauses (if found each clause is processed separately), personal pronouns such as He/She, subject pronouns(such as who) and certain words which are used often while using proverbs in the paragraph for example: (realized, said, told, etc). According to the various possibilities of the languages and probabilities of the rules, a certain grade is assigned to each criteria and sentences are evaluated accordingly.

The following three tables describe the evaluation of the sample paragraph using the rule generalization method for idiom detection.

Sentence	Clause 0.5	Tense Score Present = 2.5
There is this boy in my neighborhood.	0	Simple Present 2.5
He is Very strangely	0	Present

Sentence	Score	Tense
dressed and remains quite aloof		2.5
He has tattoos all over his body.	0	Simple Present 2.5
But you know what they say, don't judge a book by its cover.	0.5	Simple Present 2.5
I went ahead and tried to converse with this boy.	0	Past 0
And I was right, this boy indeed had a very interesting nature.	0	Simple Past 0
He was just a teenager in his growing phase.	0	Past Continuos 0
That is when I realized, to understand others we need to put ourselves in other people's shoes.	0.5	Simple Present 2.5

Table 2: Evaluation of sample paragraph using the tense rule and clause rule generalization method

Table 2 checks each statement in the paragraph for the presence of a clause and the tense of the statement. The scoring of the criteria is currently done manually on the 5 point scale depending on how much a rule can actually determine the presence of a proverb. The presence of clause is given the score of 0.5 because, simply presence of clause is very common in a paragraph and in itself is not a very good indication of the statement being a proverb. Whereas, if a statement is in present tense, possibility of statement being a proverb is increased, therefore a score of 2.5 is given if the statement is in present tense. Similarly the scores have been assigned for each criterion according to the capacity of the given criteria to determine the statement as a proverb. Table 3 checks each statement for the presence of a clause along with presence of certain words common in the idiomatic sentences. It also checks presence of the personal pronoun (PP) and the subject pronoun (SP) and adds or decreases the score according to the rule.

Sentence	Clause + that 1	Words: Realized, told, said, knew, say - 0.5	Voice Active - 1.5 Passive - 0	PP + SP (+1) Only PP (-1)
There is this boy in my neighborhood.	0	0	1.5	0
He is Very strangely dressed and remains quite aloof	0	0	0	-2
He has tattoos all over his body.	0	0	1.5	-2
But you know what they say, don't judge a book by its cover.	0	0.5	1.5	0
I went ahead and tried to converse with this boy.	0	0	1.5	0
And I was right, this boy indeed had a very interesting nature.	0	0	1.5	0
He was just a teenager in his growing phase.	0	0	1.5	-2
That is when I realized, to understand others we need to put ourselves in other people's shoes.	1	0.5	1.5	0

Table 3: Evaluation of sample paragraph using the active passive voice and pronouns rules

Sentence	Total Score
There is this boy in my neighborhood.	3.5
He is Very strangely dressed and remains quite aloof	0.5
He has tattoos all over his body.	2
But you know what they say, don't judge a book by its cover.	4.5
I went ahead and tried to converse with this boy.	1.5
And I was right, this boy indeed had a very interesting nature.	1.5
He was just a teenager in his growing phase.	-0.5
That is when I realized, to understand others we need to put ourselves in other people's shoes.	6

Table 4: Evaluation of sample paragraph using the rule generalization method- final total of all rule criterions

After the analysis using the generalized rules method, we have rated the sentences based on whether they follow various grammar rules usually followed by most of the idiomatic sentences. Using the classification method, we have further analyzed and rated the same statement based on the difference in its semantic context with the context of the entire paragraph. Therefore a statement getting a highest score using these two methods can be assumed to have higher probability of being an idiomatic statement.

Based on the analysis of the rule based and classification method, the total score was calculated as the combination score of the grading assigned by the two methods as shown in the following table.

Sentence	Classification method	General language rule based method	Total score
There is this boy in my neighborhood.	3.5	3.5	7
He is Very strangely dressed and remains quite aloof	3.5	0.5	4
He has tattoos all over his body.	1.5	2	3.5
But you know what they say, don' t judge a book by its cover.	3.5	4.5	8
I went ahead and tried to converse with this boy.	1.5	1.5	3
And I was right, this boy indeed had a very interesting nature.	3.5	1.5	5
He was just a teenager in his growing phase.	4.5	-0.5	4
That is when I realized, to understand others we need to put ourselves in other people' s shoes.	1.5	6	7.5

Table 5: Total score calculated by the combination score of the two methods

As we can see, the two idioms in the paragraph got detected with the highest score. A data set consisting paragraphs from different domains was tested using the similar method of implementation as mentioned above with the sample paragraph.

5. Results

Various paragraphs containing an idiomatic statement were tested based on the method specified in the implementation section. The sample data contained paragraphs of various lengths. First the classification method was applied on every statement of the paragraph and scores were assigned based on difference in categories. This was followed by the grammar rule generalization method used to test all the sentences in the same paragraph. A score was assigned based on the number and weightage of criterions that the statement follows.

It was observed that most of the proverbs were detected with the highest scoring in the analysis. While for few of the paragraphs, the above method failed to detect idioms correctly. It was also observed that as the number of idioms in a paragraph grew higher, the algorithm failed to work. But considering the fact that usually number of idioms in a paragraph is usually limited, this algorithm can be assumed to work in general for most of the cases.

6. Conclusion

This paper proposed the idea of using categorization and generalization based on rules in order to detect idioms in a given paragraph with more efficiency. The classification method included comparing the category of the entire paragraph with the category of the statement and determining the highest difference between the categories. The generalization method included algorithm to determine whether a sentence follows certain common POS based rules followed by most sentences which are idioms. This paper also proposed the use of POS tags based ontology for the storage of idioms and their corresponding translations with similar meaning in other languages.

7. Bibliographical References

Bradbury N., (2002). Transforming Experience into Tradition: Two Theories of Proverb Use and Chaucer's Practice. In Oral Tradition (Volume 17 Issue 2, 2002), pages 261-289.

Brahmaleen S., Singh A. and Goyal V., (2010). Identification of Proverbs in Hindi Text Corpus and their Translation into Punjabi. In Journal of Computer Science and Engineering, (Volume 2 Issue 1, July 2010), pages 32-37.

Coinnigh M., (2013). The Heart of Irish-Language Proverbs? An Linguo-Stylistic Analysis of Explicit Metaphor. In Proverbium: Yearbook of International Proverb Scholarship (volume 30, 2013), pages 113-150.

Dash B., (2016). Filching commonality by translation of proverb in Indian Linguistic Scene. Translation Today (Volume10, Issue-I, June 2016), pages 15-32.

Goyal V. and Priyanka, (2009). Implementation of Rule Based Algorithm for Sandhi-Vicheda of Compound Hindi Words. International Journal of Computer Science Issues, Volume 3(2009), pages 45-49.

Goyal V. and Sharma M., (2011). Extracting proverbs in machine translation from Hindi to Punjabi using regional data approach. International Journal of Computer Science and Communication (Volume 2, No. 2, July-December 2011), pages 611-613.

Mukerjee A., Soni A., and Raina A., (2006). Detecting Complex Predicates in Hindi using POS Projection across Parallel Corpora. In proceedings of Coling/ACL Workshop on Multi-Word Expressions, Sydney, July 23, 2006.

Pisharoty D., Sidhaye P., Utpat H., Wandkar S. and Sugandhi R.,(2012). Extending Capabilities of English to Marathi Machine Translator. IJCSI International Journal of Computer Science Issues, (Volume 9, Issue 3, No 3, May 2012), ISSN (Online): 16940814

Sriram V, (2005). Relative compositionality of multi-word expressions: a study of verb-noun (V-N) collocations. In Proceedings of International Joint Conference on Natural Language Processing - 2005, Jeju Island, Korea.

Sriram V and Joshi A., (2005). Measuring the relative compositionality of verb-noun (V-N) collocations by integrating features. In Proceedings of Human Language Technology Conference/Conference on

Empirical Methods in Natural Language Processing (HLT/EMNLP) - 2005, Vancouver.

Sriram V and Joshi A., (2004). Recognition of Multi-word Expressions: A Study of Verb-Noun (V-N) Collocations. In the proceedings of ICON 2004, Dec 2004, Hyderabad, pages 19-22.

Stock O., (1989). Parsing with flexibility, dynamic strategies, and idioms in mind. In Computational Linguistics (Volume 15 Issue 1, March 1989).

Tapanainen P., Piitulainen J. and Jarvinen T., (1998). Idiomatic object usage and support verbs. In the proceedings of 36th Annual Meeting of the Association for Computational Linguistics and Coling/ACL 17th International Conference on Computational Linguistics (volume 2, August 1998), pages 1289-1293, Montreal, Quebec, Canada.

Toutanova, A., Klein D., Singer Y. and Manning C., (2003). Feature-rich part-of-speech tagging with a cyclic dependency network. In Proceedings of 2003 HLT-NAACL, pages 252-259.

Toutanova, A. and Manning C., (2000). Enriching the knowledge sources used in a maximum entropy part-of-speech tagger. In Proceedings of the 2000 joint SIGDAT Conference on Empirical Methods in Natural Language Processing and Very Large Corpora (EMNLP/VLC-2000), pages 63-70.

Proceedings of the WILDRE5– 5th Workshop on Indian Language Data: Resources and Evaluation, pages 51–59
Language Resources and Evaluation Conference (LREC 2020), Marseille, 11–16 May 2020
© European Language Resources Association (ELRA), licensed under CC-BY-NC

Polish Lexicon-Grammar Development Methodology as an Example for Application to other Languages

Zygmunt Vetulani[1], Grażyna Vetulani[2]

[1,2] Adam Mickiewicz University in Poznań
[1] Faculty of Mathematics and Computer Science
[1] ul. Uniwersytetu Poznańskiego 4, 61-614, Poznań, Poland
[2] Faculty of Modern Languages and Literatures
[2] al. Niepodległości 4, 61-874, Poznań, Poland
{vetulani, gravet}@amu.edu.pl

Abstract

In the paper we present our methodology with the intention to propose it as a reference for creating lexicon-grammars. We share our long-term experience gained during research projects (past and on-going) concerning the description of Polish using this approach. The above-mentioned methodology, linking semantics and syntax, has revealed useful for various IT applications. Among other, we address this paper to researchers working on "less" or "middle-resourced" Indo-European languages as a proposal of a long term academic cooperation in the field. We believe that the confrontation of our lexicon-grammar methodology with other languages – Indo-European, but also Non-Indo-European languages of India, Ugro-Finish or Turkic languages in Eurasia – will allow for better understanding of the level of versatility of our approach and, last but not least, will create opportunities to intensify comparative studies. The reason of presenting some our works on language resources within the Wildre workshop is the intention not only to take up the challenge thrown down in the CFP of this workshop which is: "To provide opportunity for researchers from India to collaborate with researchers from other parts of the world", but also to generalize this challenge to other languages.

Keywords: language resources, lexicon-grammar, wordnet, Indian languages, non-Indoeuropean languages

1. Introduction

In the linguistic tradition a crucial role in language description was typically given to dictionaries and grammars. The oldest preserved dictionaries were in form of cuneiform tablets with Sumerian-Akkadian word-pairs and are dated 2300 BC. Grammars are "younger". Among the first were grammars for Sanskrit attributed to Yaska (6th century BC) and Pāṇini (6-5th century BC). In Europe the oldest known grammars and dictionaries date from the Hellenic period. The first one was *Art of Grammar* by Dyonisus Thrax (170-90 BCE), in use in Greek schools still some 1,500 years later. Until recently, these tools were used for the same purposes as before - teaching and translation, and *ipso facto* were supposed to be interpreted by humans. The formal rigor was considered of secondary importance. The situation changed recently with development of computer-based information technologies. For machine language processing (as machine translation, text and speech understanding, etc.) it appeared crucial to adapt language description methodology to the technology-imposed needs of precision. Being human-readable was not enough, new technological age required from grammars and dictionaries to become machine-readable. New concepts of organization of language description for better facing technological challenges emerged. One among them was the concept of lexicon-grammar.

This paper addresses two cases. First – languages with a rich linguistic tradition and valuable preexisting language resources, for which the methods described in this paper will be easily applicable and may bring interesting results.

Among Indian languages this will be the case of Sanskrit, Hindi and many other. On the other hand, a multitude of languages in use on the Indian subcontinent do not dispose of such a privileged starting position. In this case, in order to benefit from the methodology we describe in this paper, an effort must first be done to complete existing gaps. This is a hard work, and the paper, we hope will give some idea on the priorities on this way. Still, an important basic research effort will be necessary[1].

2. Why Lexicon-Grammars?

Development of computational linguistics and resulting language technologies made possible passage from the fundamental research to the development of real-scale applications. At this stage availability of rigorous, exhaustive and easy to implement language models and descriptions appeared necessary. The concept of lexicon-grammar answers to these needs. Its main idea is to link an important amount of grammatical (syntactic and semantic) information directly to respective words. Within this approach, it is natural to keep syntactic and semantic information stored as a part of lexicon entries together with other kinds of information (e.g. pragmatic). This principle applies first of all to verbs, but also to other words which "open" syntactic positions in a sentence, as e.g. certain nouns, adjectives and adverbs. Within this approach, we include into the lexicon-grammar all predicative words (i.e. words that represent the predicate in the sentence and which open the corresponding argument positions).

---

[1] We do not believe that basic linguistic research is avoidable on the base of technological solutions only. (See the historical statement addressed by Euclid of Alexandria (365 BC – 270 BC) to Ptolemy I (367 BC – 282 BC): "Sir, there is no royal road to geometry".)

The idea of lexicon-grammar is to link predicative words with possibly complete grammatical information related to these words. It was first systematically explored by Maurice Gross (Gross 1975, 1994), initially for French, then for other languages. Gross was also – to the best of our knowledge – the first to use the term lexicon-grammar (fr. *lexique-grammaire*)).

3. GENELEX project (1990-1994)

The **EUREKA** GENELEX[2] was a European initiative to realize the idea of lexicon-grammar in form of a generic model for lexicons and to propose software tools for lexicons management (Antoni-Lay et al., 1994). Anoni-Lay presents two reasons to build large-size lexicons as follows. "The first reason is that Natural Language applications keep on moving from research environments to the real world of practical applications. Since real world applications invariably require larger linguistic coverage, the number of entries in electronic dictionaries inevitably increases. The second reason lies in the tendency to insert an increasing amount of linguistic information into a lexicon. (…) In the eighties, new attempts were made with an emphasis on grammars, but an engineering problem arose: how to manage a huge set of more or less interdependent rules. The recent tendency is to organize the rules independently, to call them syntactic/semantic properties, and to store this information in the lexicon. A great part of the grammatical knowledge is put in the lexicon (…). This leads to systems with fewer rules and more complex lexicons." (ibid.).

The genericity of the GENELEX model is assured by:
- "theory

welcoming", what means openness of the GENELEX formalism to various linguistic theories (respecting the principle that its practical application will refer to some, well defined linguistic theories as a basis of the

lexicographer's research workshop). It should allow encoding phenomena described in different ways by different theories[3];
- possibility to generate various application-oriented lexicons;
- capacity of generation of lexicons apt to serve applications demanding a huge linguistic coverage.

The second important property of GENELEX besides genericity was the requirement of high precision and clarity of GENELEX-compatible lexicon-grammars.

GENELEX was first dedicated to a number of West-European languages, among other French, English, German, Italian. Although Polish[4] was not directly addressed by GENELEX, it was covered together with Czech and Hungarian by two EU projects (COPERNICUS projects CEGLEX – COPERNICUS 1032 (1995-1996) and GRAMLEX – COPERNICUS 621 (1995-1998))[5] whose objective was testing the potential of the extension of the novel GENELEX-based LT solutions to highly inflectional (as Polish) and agglutinative (as Hungarian) languages. Positive results obtained within this project demonstrated potential usefulness of the lexicon-grammar approach for so far less-resourced languages, Indo-European or not. In particular, the case of Polish demonstrated the need to take into account, within the lexicon-grammar approach, the specificity of highly inflected languages, like Lain or Sanskrit, with complex verbal and nominal morphology.

4. Lexicon-Grammar of Polish

Already in our early works on question-understanding-and-answering systems (Vetulani, Z. 1988, 1997) we capitalized the advantages of the lexicon-grammar approach. In addition to information typically provided in

---

[2] GENELEX was followed by several other EU projects, such as LE-PAROLE (1996-1998), LE-SIMPLE (1998-2000) and GRAAL (1992-1996).

[3] The GENELEX creators make a clear distinction between independence with respect to language theory, and the necessity for any particular application to be covered by some language theory compatible with the GENELEX model (this is in order to organize correctly the lexicographer's work).

[4] Polish, like all other Slavic languages, Latin and, in some respect, also Germanic languages, has a developed inflection system. Inflectional categories are case and number for nouns, gender, mood, number, person tense, and voice for verbs, case, gender, number and degree for adjectives, degree alone for adverbs, etc. Examples of descriptive categories are gender for nouns and aspect for verbs. The verbal inflection system (called conjugation) is simpler than in most Romance or Germanic languages but still complex enough to precisely situate action or narration on the temporal axis. The second of the two main paradigms (called declension) is the nominal one. It is based on the case and number oppositions. The declension

system of Polish strongly marks Polish syntax; as the declension case endings characterize the function of the word within the sentence, therefore the word order is more free than in, e.g., Romance or Germanic languages where the position of the word in a sentence is meaningful. Main representatives of the Polish declension system are nouns, but also adjectives, numerals, pronouns and participles. Polish inflected forms are created by combining various grammatical morphemes with stems. These morphemes are mainly prefixes and suffixes (endings). Endings are considered as the typical inflection markers and traditional classifications into inflection classes are based on ending configurations. Endings may fulfil various syntactic and semantic functions at the same time. A large variety of inflectional categories for most of parts of speech is the reason why inflection paradigms are complex and long in Polish. For example, the nominal paradigm has 14 positions, the length of the verbal paradigm is 37 and the length of the adjectival one is 84 (Vetulani, G. 2000).

[5] Some of the outcomes of these project are described in (Vetulani, G. 2000).

dictionaries we managed to explore structural, as well as morpho-syntactic-and-semantic information directly stored with predicative words, i.e. words which are surface manifestation of sentence predicates. In Polish, as in many (all?) Indo-European languages, these are typically verbs, but also nouns, adjectives, participles and adverbs. The content of lexicon-grammar entries informs about the structure of minimal complete elementary sentences supported by the predictive words, both simple and compound. This information may be precious in order to substantially speed-up sentence processing[6] (see e.g. Vetulani, Z. 1997). Taking this into account, the text processing stage requires a new kind of language resource which is electronic lexicon-grammar. In opposition to small text processing demo systems developed so far, this requirement appears demanding when starting to build real size applications within the concept of predicate-argument approach to syntax of elementary sentences that we applied in our rule-based text analyzers and generators. The rule-based approach dominating still at the turn of the centuries remains important in all cases where high processing precision is essential.

Concerning digital language resources Polish was clearly under-resourced at those days, however with a good starting position due to well-developed traditional language descriptions. For example, since 1990s the high quality lexicon-grammar in the form of Generative Syntactic Dictionary of Polish Verbs (Polański 1980-1982) was to our disposal. This impressive resource of 7,000 most widely used Polish simple verbs, being addressed first of all to human users, was hardly computer-readable. As simplified example of an entry we propose the description of the polysemic predicative verb POLECIEĆ (meaning *to fly*). One of its meanings is represented by the following entry (lines a – d):

(a) POLECIEĆ (English: FLY)[7]
(b) $NP_{Nominative}+NPI+(NP_{Ablative})+(NP_{Adlative})$
(c) $NP_{Nominative}$ [human]; $NP_{Instrumental}$ [flying object]; $NP_{Ablative}$ [location]; $NP_{Adlative}$ [location]
(d) Examples:
..., *Ja(NP_N) z Warszawy (NP_{Abl}) do Francji (NP_{Adl})*
POLECĘ samolotem (NPI), ...
..., *I (NP_N) WILL FLY from Warsaw(NP_{Abl}) to France(NP_{Adl}) by plane(NP_I)), ... ,*
where:

(a) is the entry identifier (verb in infinitive)
(b) is the *sentential scheme* showing the syntactic structure and syntactic requirements of the verb with respect to obligatory and facultative (in brackets) arguments (it may be considered as a simple sentence pattern)
(c) is the specification of semantic requirements of the verb for obligatory and facultative arguments (ontology concepts in brackets)
(d) provides some use examples

The formalism ignores details of the surface realization of meaning, such as case, gender, number, etc. of words. The pioneering and revelatory work of Polański was limited to simple verbs but both method and formalism perfectly support compound constructions. What follows is an example of an entry for a verb-noun collocation composed of a predicatively empty *support verb (light verb* in the terminology used by Fillmore (2002) together with a predicative noun which plays the function of compound verb in the sentence *Orliński and Kubiak odbyli lot z Warszawy do Tokio samolotem in a Breguet 19 w roku 1926 (In 1926, Oliński flew/made a flight from Warsaw to Tokyo in a Breguet 19).*

The dictionary entry for ODBYĆ LOT in the above format will be:
(a') ODBYĆ LOT (English: FLY)[8]
(b') $NP_N +NP_I+(NP_{Abl})+(NP_{Adl})+(DATE)$
(c') NP_N [human]; NP_I [flying object]; NP_{Abl} [location]; NP_{Adl} [location]; DATE [year].

Information contained in lexicon-grammar entries appeared very useful in various NLP tasks. For example, an important part of information useful for simple sentence understanding may be easily accessed through basic forms of words identified in the sentence. Parts (b) and (c) of the dictionary entries for the identified predicative word will help to make precise hypotheses[9] about the syntactic-semantic pattern of the sentence.

Despite their merits, the traditional syntactic lexicons, as is the above presented Syntactic Generative Dictionary, are not sufficient to supply all necessary linguistic information to solve all language processing problems. The case of highly inflected Polish (but also other Slavonic languages, Latin, German etc.) demonstrates the need of precise and complete description of morphology. For Polish we delivered within the project POLEX (1994-1996) a large

---

[6] E.g. in heuristic parsing in order to limit the grammar search space explored by the parser (Vetulani, Z. 1997).

[7] "We do not claim that the set of semantic features we propose is exhaustive and final. Besides features commonly accepted we considered necessary to introduce such distinction words as nouns designing plants, elements, information etc.", cf. (Polański 1992).

[8] "We do not claim that the set of semantic features we propose is exhaustive and final. Besides features commonly accepted we considered necessary to introduce such distinction words as nouns designing plants, elements, information etc.", cf. (Polański 1992).

[9] The concept of *syntactic hypothesis* is crucial for our methods of heuristic parsing making a right choice of hypothesis about the sentence structure may considerably reduce the parsing cost (in time and space). With good heuristics, in some cases it is possible to reduce the grammatical search space considerably and as a result turning the nondeterministic parser into a *de facto* deterministic one. We explored this idea with very good effects in our rule-based question-answering systems POLINT (see e.g. section Preanalysis in (Vetulani, Z. 1997).

electronic dictionary (Vetulani, Z. et al. 1998 ; Vetulani, Z. 2000) of over 120,000 entries.[10] This resource is easily machine treatable and was used as Polish Lexicon-Grammar complement.

5.   Citing « PolNet – Polish Wordnet » as lexical ontology

Within our real-size application projects[11] we extensively used a lexical ontology to represent meaning of text messages. Absence on the market of ontologies reflecting the world conceptualization typical of Polish speakers pushed us to build from scratch PolNet – Polish Wordnet, lexical database of the type of Princeton WordNet[12]. In Princeton WordNet like systems basic entities are classes of synonyms (synsets) related by some relations of which the most important are hyponymy and hyperonymy. Synsets may be considered as ontology concepts with the advantage of being direcly linked to words.

We started the PolNet project in 2006[13] at the Department of Computer Linguistics and Artificial Intelligence of Adam Mickiewicz University and its progress continues. The resource development procedure was based on the exploration of good traditional dictionaries of Polish and the use of available language corpora (e.g. IPI PAN Corpus; cf. Przepiórkowski, 2004) in order to select the most important vocabulary, for the purpose of the application expanded with the application specific terminology[14]. Development of PolNet was organized in an incremental way, starting with general and frequently used vocabulary[15]. By 2008, the initial PolNet version based on noun synsets related by hyponymy/hyperonymy relations was already rich enough to serve as core lexical ontology for real-size application developed in the project (POLINT-112-SMS system cf. Vetulani, Z. et al. 2010). Further extension with verbs and collocations, operated after the 2009, contributed to transform PolNet into a lexicon-grammar intended to ease implementation of AI systems with natural language competence and other NLP-related tasks.

```
<SYNSET>
<ID>PL_PK-518264818</ID>
<POS>n</POS>
<DEF>instytucja zajmująca się kształceniem; educational institution </DEF>
<SYNONYM>
<LITERAL lnote="U1" sense="1">szkoła</LITERAL>     % szkoła=school
<LITERAL lnote="U1" sense="5">buda</LITERAL>
<LITERAL lnote="U1" sense="1">szkółka</LITERAL>

.....

</SYNONYM>
<USAGE>Skończyć szkołę</USAGE>
<USAGE>Kierownik szkoły</USAGE>

.....

<ILR type="hypernym" link="POL-2141701467">instytucja oświatowa:1</ILR>
<RILR type="hypernym" link="POL-2141575802">uczelnia:1,szkoła wyższa:1,wszechnica:1</RILR>
<RILR type="hypernym" link="POL-2141603029">szkoła średnia:1</RILR

.....

<STAMP>Weronika 2007-07-15 12:07:38</STAMP>
<CREATED>Weronika 2007-07-15 12:07:38</CREATED>
</SYNSET>
```

Fig. 1. The PolNet v.0.1 entry for (school *szkoła*) (the sysnset{szkoła:1,buda:5, szkółka:1,....}; indices 1, 5, ... refer to the particular sense of the word *szkoła*) (Vetulani, Z. 2012)

---

[10] POLEX dictionary is distributed through ELDA (www.elda.fr) under ISLRN 147-211-031-223-4.

[11] For detailed description of language resources and tools used to develop POLINT-112-SMS system (2006-2010) and the specification of its language competence see (Vetulani, Z. et al., 2010).

[12] Princeton WordNet (Miller et al., 1990) was (and continue to be) widely used as a formal ontology to design and implement systems with language understanding functionality. In order to respect specific Polish conceptualization of world, we decided to build PolNet from scratch rather than merely translate Princeton WordNet into Polish. Building from scratch is more costly, but the reward we get in return was an ontology well corresponding to the conceptualization reflected in the language. We do not recommend "translation-based" construction of a wordnet for languages socio-culturally remote with respect to the source wordnet language, in particular for language pairs spoken by socio-culturally different communities.

[13] Another large wordnet-like lexical database for Polish started at about the same time at the Technical University in Wrocław (Piasecki et al. 2009). It was however based on different methodological approach.

[14] Lack of appropriate terminological dictionaries forced us to collect experimental corpora and extract missing terminology manually (Walkowska, 2009; Vetulani, Z. et al. 2010).

[15] See (Vetulani, Z. et al., 2007) for the PolNet development algorithm.

6. From PolNet to a Lexicon-Grammar for Polish

6.1 First step – simple verbs

Integration of the lexicon-grammar approach to syntax with the word-based approach to ontology was the idea behind the evolution from the PolNet 1.0 (2011) to the PolNet 3.0 (and further). This idea was implemented through expansion of the initial PolNet of nouns with other parts of speech, first of all with simple verbs, second by predicative multi-word constructions.[16]

The first step was extension of PolNet with simple verbs. This extension was operated relatively fast due to high quality of the Polański's Generative Dictionary. However, as a machine-readable version of this dictionary did not exist, the work of building verb synsets was to be done fully manually by experienced lexicographers.

In (Vetulani, Z. & Vetulani, G., 2014) we presented the concept of a verb synset as follows: "In opposition to nouns, where the focus is on the relations between concepts (represented by synsets), and in particular on hyperonymy/hyponymy relations, for verbs the main interest is in relating verbal synsets (representing predicative concepts) to noun synsets (representing general concepts) in order to show what connectivity constraints corresponding to the particular argument positions are. (…) Synonymous will be only such verb+meaning pairs in which the same *semantic roles*[17] take the same concepts as value (necessary but not sufficient). In particular, the valency structure of a verb is one of indices of meaning (members of a sysnset share the valency structure)."

Synsets for simple verbs appeared already in the first public release of PolNet in 2011 (PolNet 1.0) (Vetulani, Z. et al. 2016). (See Fig. 2, below). Already this first extension steps in turning PolNet into a lexicon-grammar permitted us to make a smart use of PolNet enriched with lexicon-grammar features to control parsing execution by heuristics[18] in order to speed-up parsing due to additional information gathered at the pre-parsing stage. The effect of substantially reducing the processing time was due to the reduction of search space.

6.2 Next step – compound verbs

The next steps consisting in expanding the initial PolNet-based lexicon-grammar with compound verbs were more demanding. The first reason for that was scarcity of dictionaries of compound words (phrasemes, or special multi-word constructions like collocations), both for general vocabulary and for domain-specific terminology (with exception of some domains). Another problem for almost all languages is insufficiency of serious research concerning syntax, semantics and pragmatics for compound words. These two problem remain to be solved by the concerned teams.

6.2.1 Lexicographical basic research on verb-noun collocations

Systematic studies[19] of Polish verb-noun collocations were initiated in the 1990s by Grażyna Vetulani. In the first phase they consisted in "manual" examination of over 40,000 of Polish nouns on "Słownik Języka Polskiego PWN" (Szymczak, 1995). This operation resulted with selection of over 7,500 abstract nouns liable to predicative use. Among them, a subset of over 2850 typical predicative nouns was identified as of primary importance to start extending a verbs-only initial lexicon-grammar with verb-nouns collocation (Vetulani, G. 2000). This class is the most important, but also the most heterogeneous, thereby hard to processing.[20] It is composed of names of activities and behavior, names of actions, techniques, methods, operations, states, processes, human activities, nature of objects of various kinds, etc. All these predicative nouns select their (predicatively empty) support verbs, simple or compound, and arguments. It is typical of this class that predicative nous accept more than one (sometimes many) support verbs to form compound verbs (verb-noun collocations) with the valency structure of the noun. In most cases these collocations will be synonyms and therefore will belong to the same synset. However, the difference between collocations due to the selection of different support verbs will be visible at the pragmatic level.

The initial step consisting in dictionary-based acquisition of collocations was concluded by the publication of the first version of Verb-Noun Collocation Dictionary (Vetulani, G. 2000) of over 5,400 entries. The main efforts have been made to retrieve collocations from the traditional dictionary, to elaborate a human-and-machine processible format of entries and to produce dictionary entries.

What follows is an example of a dictionary entry in the format described in (Vetulani, G. 2000) :

---

[16] For Polish, construction of PolNet entries for simple nouns and verbs was relatively easy because of availability of good quality dictionaries, however for many of the so called *less-resourced languages* this task will be challenging.

[17] See (Palmer 2009).

[18] A well-constructed heuristic permits – on the basis of morphological and valency information combined with the switch technique of Vetulani, Z. (1994) – to reduce the complexity of parsing down to linear in an important number of cases.

[19] Cf. (Vetulani, G. and Vetulani, Z. 2012) for this paragraph.

[20] Other identified classes of predicative nouns are: feature names (over 2,800), names of frequent diseases (over 250), names of occupations or popular professions (over 1,400), and other (e.g. nouns supported by *event verbs*); notice that particular nouns may be polysemic and may belong to more than one class (Vetulani, G. 2000).

aluzja, f/ *(allusion)*

- czynić(Acc,pl)/N1do(Gen),   *(to make ~s to sth)*
- robić(Acc,sing)/N1do(Gen),   *(to make an ~ to sth)*
- pozwalać sobie na(Acc,pl)/N1do(Gen) *(to dare to make ~s to sth)*

where Acc and Gen stand respectively for declension cases of respectively accusativus and genitivus.

The second step was operated between 2000 and 2012. Its starting point was the dictionary of some 5,400 entries for more than 2850 predicative nouns (in what follows we call it *basic resource; BR*). Its main objective was a substantial improvement of the earlier results on the basis of large text corpus of Polish and appropriate processing tools. Analysis of the results obtained by the year 2000 brought to evidence insufficiency of methods used so far, as traditional dictionaries were not sufficiently large to contain all frequently used collocations. To obtain a satisfactory balanced coverage it was necessary to make use of corpora. Machine-assisted investigation of the text IPI PAN corpus (Przepiórkowski 2004) permitted to triple the number of collocation entries for the same basis of slightly more than 2,800 predicative words. To get this result we first proposed an algorithm for computer-assisted corpus-based acquisition of new collocations (Vetulani, G. et al., 2008), where by "new" collocations we mean those attested in a corpus, but absent in the BR. The main idea of this algorithm is to transform the rough corpus data in a way to substantially reduce the collocation-retrieval time with respect to fully manual retrieval procedure.

The input resources for the algorithm were:
1) Basic Resource of 2878 predicative noun entries (Vetulani, G. 2000).
2) The public available part of the IPI PAN corpus (Przepiórkowski, 2004) without morphological (and any other kind of) annotations.
The algorithm was organized into four parts:
- preparatory steps on the input data (preparation of search patterns)
- the main part which is a concordances generator to retrieve fragments of texts which match the patterns,

- clustering of text fragments obtained from the concordancer part with respect to predicative nouns (BR) and returning "support-verb candidates" (SVC) to be identified or refused as support verbs.
- manually processing (cleaning) support-verbs-candidates (SVC) in order to eliminate worthless selections (large majority).

This algorithm was further improved by the same team (Vetulani, G. et al. 2008; Vetulani, G. 2010) and applied to the input data. This modified algorithm is composed of the following five steps (to be run consecutively).

Step 1. Extraction from the corpus of contexts with high probability to contain verb-noun collocations and detection of verbs-candidates to be qualified as support verbs (automatically).

Step 2. Manual analysis by lexicographers of the list of verbs-candidates obtained in the Step 1 in order to eliminate apparently bad choices.

Step 3. Automatic extraction of contexts in form of concordances containing verb-noun pairs (selected through steps 1-3) as concordance centers.

Step 4. Reading of the concordances by lexicographers, qualification of verb-noun pairs as collocations and their morpho-syntactic descriptions (manual).

Step 5. Verification and final formatting.

The method we used permitted to reduce (~ 100 times) the processing cost (estimation on a 5% sample).

As result of the application of this algorithm we obtained an electronic dictionary of over 14,600 entries for over 2,878 predicative nouns.

6.2.2 Introduction of verb-noun collocations to PolNet

During the period from 2009 (PolNet 0.1) to 2011(PolNet 1.0) PolNet grew as a result of addition of some 1,500 synsets for 900 simple verbs corresponding to approximately 2,900 word+meaning pairs (Vetulani, Z. and Vetulani, G. 2014). Further extension from PolNet 1.0 to PolNet 2.0 consisted in addition of 1,200 new collocation synsets corresponding to 600 predicative nouns[21].

POS: v ID: 3441

Synonyms: {pomóc:1, pomagać:1, **udzielić pomocy**:1, **udzielać pomocy:1**} *(to help)*

Definition: *"to participate in sb's work in order to help him/her"*

VALENCY:

- Agent(N)_Benef(D)
- Agent(N)_Benef(D) Action('w'+NA(L))
- Agent(N)_Benef(D) Manner
- Agent(N)_Benef(D) Action('w'+NA(L)) Manner

Usage: Agent(N)_Benef(D); "Pomogłam jej." (*I helped her*)

Usage: Agent(N)_Benef(D) Action('w'+NA(L)); "Pomogłam jej w robieniu lekcji." (*I helped her in doing homework)*

Usage: Agent(N)_Benef(D) Manner Action('w'+NA(L));

"Chętnie udzieliłam jej pomocy w lekcjach." (*I helped her willingly doing her homework*)

---

[21] Notice that the number of collocations is higher than the number of predicative nouns, this is due to the fact that the same predicative noun may be supported by several support verbs.

| Usage: Agent(N)_Benef(D) Manner; |
| "Chętnie jej pomagałam." (*I used to help her willingly*) |
| Semantic_role: [Agent] {człowiek:1, homo sapiens:1, istota ludzka:1, ...} (*{man:1,...,human being:1,...}*) |
| Semantic_role: [Benef] {człowiek:1, homo sapiens:1, istota ludzka:1, ...} (*{man:1,...,human being:1,...}*) |
| Semantic_role: [Action] {czynność:1} (*{activity:1}*) |
| Semantic_role: [Manner] {CECHA_ADVERB_JAKOŚĆ:1} (*qualitative adverbial*) |

Fig. 2. Simplified DEBVisDic[22] presentation of a PolNet synset {pomóc:1, pomagać:1, **udzielić pomocy**:1, **udzielać pomocy:1**} containing both simple verbs (*pomóc*) and collocations (udzielić pomocy) (Vetulani, Z. and Kochanowski, 2014).

Fig. 2. presents the way PolNet makes use of the idea of semantics adapted after Filmore (1977) and Palmer (2009), and shows the semantic roles Agent, Beneficient, Action, Manner together with their values being noun synsets.

The passage to PolNet 2.0 opened up new application opportunities but also pushed us to re-consider the fundamental problem of synonymy for predicative words and to base it on the concept of valency structure. As valency structure of a verb is one of the formal indices of meaning, it should be considered as an attribute of a synset, i.e. all synset's members should share the valency structure. Strict application of this principle results in relatively fine granularity of the verb section of the PolNet (Vetulani, Z., Vetulani, G. 2015).

PolNet 3.0 is the last documented version of the resource. In order to obtain this new version, PolNet 2.0 was submitted to refining and cleaning operations. For the refinement operation it was assumed that the category of language register is a part of the meaning. The totality of PolNet 2.0 synsets was revised in order to split these synsets into register-uniform sub-synsets. Inclusion of register related information, up to our best knowledge until now not practiced in other wordnets, opens new application possibilities e.g. for refinement of text generation quality.

The version PolNet 3.0 has already been user-tested as a resource for modeling semantic similarity between words (Kubis, 2015).

	PolNet 0.1 (2009)	PolNet 1.0 (2011)	PolNet 2.0 (2013)	PolNet 3.0 (2016)
Nouns	10,629	11,700	11,700	12,011
Simple verbs	---	1,500	1,500	3,645
Collocations	---	---	1,200	1,908

Table. 1. Growth of the PolNet's main parts (in numer of synsets) (Vetulani, Z. et al. 2016). Notice: This table does not represent the effort invested in the development of PolNet as an important deal of work was engaged in the wordnet cleaning operations.

7. Conclusion and further work

Undoubtedly English constitutes an absolute reference point for languages classification in terms of adaptation of their description to technological needs as well as in terms of richness of tools and language resources necessary for industries to develop language technologies. At the very bottom of the hierarchy we find a significant number of languages for which it is not needed (or realistic) to develop such technologies. In the middle we locate quite a big number of languages set down as "less-resourced". Until recently the Polish language was categorized within this group. Currently we locate there some European minority languages as well as some languages from countries, by the way highly technologically developed, such as India for instance. Among other, we address this paper to researchers working on "less" or "middle-resourced" Indo-European languages as a proposal of a long term academic cooperation in the field, within which we will share experience with our partners in the area explored in this article. We believe that the confrontation of our methodology with other languages, also non-Indo-European languages of India, Ugro-Finish or Turkic in Europe and Asia, will allow for better understanding of the level of versatility of our solutions and, last but not least, will create conditions for a close cooperation.

The PolNet enlargement with verbal components required an important investment of lexicographers' work. Lexicon-Grammar for Polish is still in progress, but what has been done until now is largely sufficient to give a good insight in the nature of linguistic and engineering problems to be done by the project executors or by people aiming to undertake similar tasks for other languages. In the course of the above-mentioned works on Lexicon-Grammar for Polish we have identified a range of factors that appeared necessary to be taken into account in order to realize our project. At the beginning of our works we could dispose only of the following resources:

- traditional or in some cases electronic language resources such as: dictionaries, thesauri, lexicons
- representative and large texts corpora,
- traditional or formalized grammatical descriptions,
- IT tools for processing the above-mentioned resources.

In the lack of adequate resources the project began with building-up the lexical database of wordnet type, initially

---

[22] DEBVisDic is a tool we used for edition and maintenance of PolNet entries (Pala, K. et al.).

from nouns only, through inclusion in the next phase simple predicative verbs, and finally verb-noun collocations (with a predicative noun).

The enlargement of the initial, noun-based version of the PolNet database consisted in introducing predicative elements by, *inter alia*:

-   identifying predicative simple and complex words: description of the predicate-valency structure for simple and complex predicative expressions and proposing a format for predicative synsets,
-   generating predicative synsets and linking with respective arguments (noun synsets).

Problems to be solved / elaborated are as follow:

-   synonymy, granularity,
-   aspects,
-   meaning shift, diachrony,
-   other relations:
    o   hyponymia/hyperonmy
    o   meronymy
    o   passive and active verb opposition
-   morphology,
-   pragmatic issues:
    o   language registers,
    o   regionalisms.

Another hot issue for existing lexicon-grammar systems of different languages is to align them with each other. It is a demanding task, often hardly feasible due to different conceptualization of the world in various communities, and reflected in respective languages.

The reason of presenting some our works on language resources within the Wildre workshop is the intention to encourage taking up the challenge thrown in the CFP of this workshop which is: "To provide opportunity for researchers from India to collaborate with researchers from other parts of the world".

8. Acknowledgements

The succesful achievement of projects reported in this overview would be impossible without the collaboration of numerous institutions and notable individuals. We would like to express our gratitude to the many academic collaborators, student volunteers, and colleagues across Academia and various partner, who generously invested their time and expertise to make this research possible.

9. Bibliographical References

Antoni-Lay, M-H. Francopoulo, G. Zaysser, L. (1994). *A Generic Model for Reusable Lexicons: The Genelex Project*, In *Literary and Linguistic Computing*, vol. 9, no 1, Oxford University Press, 47-54.

Fillmore, Ch.J. (1977). *The need for a frame semantics in linguistics. Statistical Methods in Linguistics*. Ed. Hans Karlgren. Scriptor.

Fillmore, Ch.J. (2002). Seeing Arguments through Transparent Structures, *Proceedings of Third International Conference on Language Resources and Evaluation, Proceedings,* Vol. III, Las Palmas, 787–791.

Gross, M. (1975). *Méthodes en syntaxe,* Paris: Hermann.

Gross, M. (1994). Constructing Lexicon-grammars. In Atkins and Zampolli (eds.) *Computational Approaches to the Lexicon,* Oxford University Press, p. 213-263.

Kubis, M. (2015). A semantic similarity measurement tool for WordNet-like databases. In Z. Vetulani and J. Mariani (Eds), *Proceedings of the 7th Language and Technology Conference, Poznań, Poland, 27-29 November 2015.* FUAM, Poznań, pp. 150 – 154.

Miller, G. A, Beckwith, R., Fellbaum, C.D., Gross, D., Miller, K. (1990). WordNet: An online lexical database. Int. J. Lexicograph. 3, 4, 235–244.

Palmer, M. (2009). Semlink: Linking PropBank, VerbNet and FrameNet. In *Proceedings of the Generative Lexicon Conference. Sept. 2009, Pisa, Italy.*

Polański K. (Ed.) (1980-1992). *Słownik syntaktyczno-generatywny czasowników polskich,* vol. I-IV, Ossolineum, Wrocław, 1980-1990, vol. V, Instytut Języka Polskiego PAN, Kraków, 1992.

Piasecki M., Szpakowicz S., Broda B. (2009). *A Wordnet from the Ground Up*, Oficyna Wydawnicza Politechniki Wrocławskiej, Wrocław.

Przepiórkowski, A. (2004). *Korpus IPI PAN. Wersja wstępna (The IPI PAN Corpus: Preliminary version).* IPI PAN, Warszawa.

Szymczak, M. (red.) (1995). *Słownik Języka Polskiego,* PWN, Warszawa.

Vetulani, G. & Vetulani, Z. & Obrębski, T. (2008). Verb-Noun Collocation SyntLex Dictionary - Corpus-Based Approach, In: *Proceedings of 6th International Conference on Language Resources and Evaluation, May 26 - June 1, 2008, Marrakech, Morocco (Proceedings)*, ELRA, Paris.

Vetulani, G. (2000). *Rzeczowniki predykatywne języka polskiego. W kierunku syntaktycznego słownika rzeczowników predykatywnych na tle porównawczym,* Adam Mickiewicz University Press: Poznań.

Vetulani, G. (2010). *Kolokacje werbo-nominalne jako samodzielne jednostki języka polskiego. Syntaktyczny słownik kolokacji werbo-nominalych języka polskiego na potrzeby zastosowań informatycznych. Część I.* Adam Mickiewicz University Press: Poznań.

Vetulani, G. and Vetulani Z. (2012). Dlaczego Leksykon-Gramatyka? In: Anna Dutka-Mańkowska, Anna Kieliszczyk, Ewa Pilecka (ed.), *Grammaticis unitis. Mélanges offers à Bohdan Krzysztof Bogacki,* Wydawnictwa Uniwersytetu Warszawskiego. 308-316.

Vetulani, Z. (1988). PROLOG Implementation of an Access in Polish to a Data Base, w: Studia z automatyki, XII, PWN, 1988, pp. 5-23.

Vetulani, Z. (1994). SWITCHes for making Prolog more Dynamic Programming Language, Logic Programming, The Newsletter of the Association for Logic Programming, vol 7/1, February 1994, pp. 10.

Vetulani, Z. and Jassem, K. (1994) Linguistically Based Optimisation of a TDDF Parsing Algorithm of the NL system POLINT. In: Dieter W. Halwachs (Eds.), Akten des 28 Linguistischen Kolloquiums, Graz - 1993 (Linguistische Arbeiten 321), Max Niemeyer Verlag, Tübingen, 1994, pp. 321-326.

Vetulani, Z. (1997). A system for Computer Understanding of Texts, in: R. Murawski, J. Pogonowski (Eds.), *Euphony and Logos.* Poznań Studies in the Philosophy of the Sciences and the Humanities, vol. 57. Rodopi, Amsterdam-Atlanta, 387-416; ISBN: 90-420-0382-0; ISSN 0303-8157.

Vetulani, Z. , Walczak, B., Obrębski, T., Vetulani, G. (1998). *Unambiguous coding of the inflection of Polish nouns and its application in the electronic dictionaries - format POLEX / Jednoznaczne kodowanie fleksji rzeczownika polskiego i jego zastosowanie w słownikach elektronicznych - format POLEX,* Adam Mickiewicz University Press, Poznań.

Vetulani, Z. (2000); Electronic Language Resources for POLISH: POLEX, CEGLEX and GRAMLEX. In: M. Gavrilidou et al. (Eds.) *Second International Conference on Language Resources and Evaluation, Athens, Greece, 30.05.-2.06.2000, (Proceedings),* ELRA, pp. 367-374.

Vetulani, Z., Walkowska, J., Obrębski, T., Konieczka, P., Rzepecki P., Marciniak, J. (2007). PolNet - Polish WordNet project algorithm, in: Z. Vetulani (ed.) *Proceedings of the 3rd Language and Technology Conference: Human Language Technologies as a Challenge for Computer Science and Linguistics, October 5-7, 2007, Poznań, Poland,* Wyd. Poznańskie, Poznań, ISBN 978-83-7177-407-2, pp. 172-176.

Vetulani, Z., Marcinak, J., Obrębski, T., Vetulani, G., Dabrowski, A., Kubis, M., Osiński, J., Walkowska, J., Kubacki, P., Witalewski, K. (2010). *Zasoby językowe i technologie przetwarzania tekstu. POLINT-112-SMS jako przykład aplikacji z zakresu bezpieczeństwa publicznego (in Polish) (Language resources and text processing technologies. POLINT-112-SMS as example of homeland security oriented application),* ISBN 978-83-232-2155-5, ISSN 1896-379X, Adam Mickiewicz University Press: Poznań.

Vetulani, Z. (2012). Wordnet Based Lexicon Grammar for Polish. *Proceedings* of the Eight International Conference on Language Resources and Evaluation (*LREC 2012*), May 23-25, 2012. Istanbul, Turkey, (Proceedings), ELRA: Paris. ISBN 978-2-9517408-7-7, pp. 1645-1649. http://www.lrec-conf.org/ proceedings/ lrec2012/index.html

Vetulani, Z., Kochanowski, B. (2014). "PolNet - Polish Wordnet" project: PolNet 2.0 – a short description of the release, in: Heili Orav, Christiane Fellbaum, Piek Vossen (eds.) *GWC 2014. Proc. of the Seventh Global Wordnet Conference 2014, Tartu, Estonia,* Global Wordnet Association, pp. 400-404.

Vetulani, Z., Vetulani, G. (2014). Through Wordnet to Lexicon Grammar, in. Fryni Kakoyianni Doa (Ed.). *Penser le lexique grammaire: perspectives actuelles,* Editions Honoré Champion, Paris, pp. 531-543.

Vetulani, Z., Vetulani, G., Kochanowski, B. (2016). "Recent Advances in Development of a Lexicon-Grammar of Polish: PolNet 3.0". In: Nicolette Calzolari et al. (Eds.), *Proceedings of the Tenth International Conference on Language Resources and Evaluation (LREC 2016),* European Language Resources Association (ELRA), Paris, France, ISBN 978-2-9517408-9-1, pp. 2851-2854, hal-01414304.

Walkowska, J. (2009). *Gathering and Analysis of a Corpus of Polish SMS Dialogues.* [in:] Kłopotek, M. A., et al. (Eds.), Challenging Problems of Science. Computer Science. Recent Advances in Intelligent Information Systems Academic Publishing.

10. Language Resource References

Zygmunt Vetulani (2014). POLEX Polish Lexicon. ISLRN 147-211-031-223-4, distributed via ELRA, http://catalog.elra.info/en-us/repository/browse/ELRA-L0074/.

Zygmunt Vetulani (2016). PolNet – Polish Wordnet. ISLRN 944-121-942-407-9. To be found at http://www.islrn.org/resources/944-121-942-407-9/.

Proceedings of the WILDRE5– 5ᵗʰ Workshop on Indian Language Data: Resources and Evaluation, pages 60–65
Language Resources and Evaluation Conference (LREC 2020), Marseille, 11–16 May 2020
© European Language Resources Association (ELRA), licensed under CC-BY-NC

Abstractive Text Summarization for Sanskrit Prose: A Study of Methods and Approaches

Shagun Sinha, Girish Nath Jha
School of Sanskrit and Indic Studies
Jawaharlal Nehru University, New Delhi
{shagunsinha5, girishjha}@gmail.com

Abstract

The authors present a work-in-progress in the field of Abstractive Text Summarization (ATS) for Sanskrit Prose – a first attempt at ATS for Sanskrit (SATS). We will evaluate recent approaches and methods used for ATS and argue for the ones to be adopted for Sanskrit prose considering the unique properties of the language. There are three goals of SATS - to make manuscript summaries, to enrich the semantic processing of Sanskrit, and to improve the information retrieval systems in the language. While Extractive Text Summarization (ETS) is an important method, the summaries it generates are not always coherent. For qualitative coherent summaries, ATS is considered a better option by scholars. This paper reviews various ATS/ETS approaches for Sanskrit and other Indian Languages done till date. In the preliminary overview, authors conclude that of the two available approaches - structure-based and semantics-based - the latter would be viable owing to the rich morphology of Sanskrit. Moreover, a graph-based method may also be suitable. The second suggested method is the supervised-learning method. The authors also suggest attempting cross-lingual summarization as an extension to this work in future.
Keywords: Abstractive Text Summarization, Sanskrit Prose, Computational Linguistics

1. Introduction

Text Summarization (TS) is a core area of study under Computational Linguistics (CL) and Natural Language Processing (NLP) for generation of coherent text summaries. One of the earliest works was by Luhn (1958) from IBM where he proposed to create summaries of the abstracts of scientific papers. TS has also been developed for a number of Indian Languages (ILs). Extractive text summarization (ETS) and abstractive text summarization (ATS) are two primary approaches that focus on summarizing IL internet content, newspaper articles, research papers, official documents etc (Sankar et al., 2011; Embar et al., 2013; Talukder et al., 2019; Gupta & Lehal, 2011; so on). Sanskrit is studied in various forms today mostly as a compositional language preserving several million texts of great intellectual value. The issues of text availability, readability and the need to access the knowledge in it have presented a huge requirement for ATS and related research for Sanskrit. The capacity of Sanskrit to infinitely condense an expression with recurrent usage of concatenating techniques like euphonic combinations (sandhi), compounding (samasa), scrambling, verb elision for prosody etc make it difficult to arrive at the structural or collocational meaning of the expression. When creating summaries, it is important that the semantics is processed well. Doing a good ATS for Sanskrit thus becomes extremely challenging. Summarization can be categorized differently on different bases: Single versus multi-document (based on the number of documents (Jones, 1999), textual versus multimedia (based on the mode of document), extractive versus abstractive (based on the mode of the output (Afantenos et al, 2005; Moawad & Aref, 2012). This paper is the description of an ongoing work on

Sanskrit ATS (SATS) by the authors. The main contribution of this paper lies in its surveying the existing approaches to TS done for Sanskrit till date and to look at some challenges in processing Sanskrit for ATS. The paper proposes a semantic approach for any deeper processing of the texts in the language. The authors focus on single document summarization only because a multi-document ATS may be more complex due to various factors like semantic relatedness, diversity of subject matter, size etc.

2. Motivation for Sanskrit ATS

The origin and development of TS was inspired by the need to turn long English scientific texts into shorter ones (Luhn, 1958). Currently, most ideas around TS techniques under Natural Language Processing are based on the growth of the internet and the need to condense information therein (Sunitha et. al., 2016). In this backdrop, it is important to make one observation. While Sanskrit prose content on the net needs to be summarized as well, there are two key objectives of SATS which are different from those of TS in any other language of the present day:

- A large body of scientific literature is available in Sanskrit and a lot of it is in the manuscript (MS) form. The study of an MS is a far more complex and tedious process which involves editing and re-editing a historical document till the authentic content is achieved.

- SATS will require semantic analysis. This could pave the way for better semantic processing of Sanskrit. Since ATS works on the principle of 'key essence' of the text rather than extracting the suitable sentences, it could help enhance algorithms for processing the relative meaning of the words.

3. Literature Survey

Sanskrit TS so far has explored the extractive aspect only. Barve et.al. (2015) use three TS approaches to obtain text summary for Sanskrit based on a query given by the user - Average Term Frequency-Inverse Sentence Frequency (tf-isf), Vector Space Model (VSM), and Graph-Based Approach. They concluded that the VSM produced the best summary with 80% accuracy. ETS is a good approach for prose that has a high frequency of the query-word, as is seen in Barve et. al (2015). However, not all prose may yield such results. In most cases, the keyword is not always repeated but is indicated through pronouns. While query-directed extraction can be highly successful in the former, it may not be so for the latter. Besides, the ETS also faces the incoherence disadvantage as mentioned by Mishra & Gayen (2018). Abstractive approach, on the other hand, is more likely to resolve this. It 'abstracts' the essence from the text to be summarized. This leads to complexity in language processing but once successful, can result in enhanced summary quality with natural text generation. Scholars suggest that non-extractive methods generate better summaries because they reduce the information loss (Mishra & Gayen, 2018). ATS has also been found better than ETS in other work (Giuseppe & Jackie, 2008).

3.1. Major ATS approaches for Indian Languages:

Scholars have different bases for organizing the types of TS. Most of them can come under one or more of these categories:

1. Structure vs Semantic approach (Sunitha C et al., 2016),

2. Machine Learning (ML) based methods (Anh & Trang, 2019; Talukder et al., 2019) , and

3. Corpora based approach (Hasler et al., 2003)

3.1.1.

Sunitha C et. al. (2016) present a survey of the current techniques in ATS for ILs. Key approaches to ATS in ILs can be divided into two categories: Structure-based and Semantics based. Some notable works in ILs include Rich Semantic Graph approach for Hindi (Subramaniam & Dalal, 2015), Malayalam (Kabeer & Idicula, 2014), ATS through an extractive approach for Kannada (Kallimani et. el, 2014).

Structure-based approaches require the source text sentences to be collected in a predefined structure (Sunitha et al, 2016). The types of structures mentioned are Tree-based, Ontology-based, Lead and Phrase structure based, Rule based and Template-based. Each of these methods aims to collect the sentences from the source text and then generate a summary later.

In the Semantics based approach, there are three phases that lead to the summary- document input, semantic review and representation and then finally summary based on this semantic representation through Natural Language Generation (Sunitha et al., 2016). Multimodal semantic, Information Item-based and Semantic Graph (Moawad & Aref, 2012) are the methods which focus primarily on the semantic representation of the source text. It is important to note that abstraction will need semantic representation at some stage. and that ATS requires two major components always - meaning extraction and summary generation in natural language.

A closer look reveals that the ILs popularly use : the graph-, the POS-NER-, and textual position-based methods.

Of the given types, one common method is the ontology based method. Ontology refers to the 'theory of existence' or a list of all the things that exist (Russell & Norvig, 2019). A number of such summarization tools have been developed for a field-specific summarization. For example, Texminer is a tool that summarizes papers of Port and Coastal Engineering (Hipola et al, 2014); or it may be related to a particular scientific field (Luhn, 1958). We find it noteworthy that ontology is important in areas where a finite set of vocabulary pertaining to the field can be enlisted.

However, in extraction techniques in NLP, a method of ontology extraction does exist (Russell & Norvig, 2019). This may be a possible approach to get some ontology out of a general document, but its reliability for summarization purposes may have to be tested.

This brings us to the next possible approach to Indian languages text summarization which is graph-based summarization. Graphs are created out of the text document with its words as vertices and the links between them as edges (Subramaniam & Dalal, 2015). This method can be used for languages with easy tokenization availability. An additional use of WordNet is also required here.

Advanced work in graph-based methods includes 'Reduced Semantic Graph' (RSG) methods where an even more simplified version of a text's graph is generated using ontology for word-sense instantiation, concept validation and sentence-ranking (Moawad & Aref, 2012). RSG methods have been deployed for Hindi (Subramaniam & Dalal, 2015) and Malayalam (Kabeer & Idicula, 2014). The results for Hindi are reported to be up to the mark (Subramaniam & Dalal, 2015).

Due to the rich morphology of Sanskrit, a standard word-order may not be followed even in current prose. Semantic representation thus becomes an essential element. This indicates that perhaps semantic approach would yield better results.

3.1.2. Machine Learning Approaches:

One other way of classifying the TS types is the ML based approach: supervised and unsupervised methods (Majid & Fizi-Derakashi, 2015). Supervised methods require texts with their labeled summaries for training.

Unsupervised methods include graph-based, VSM, text-based. Graph-based method can be grouped with the semantic graph approach mentioned earlier. It creates a graph with concepts as vertices and the relation between them as edges (Majod, & Fizi-Derakhshi, 2015).

VSM technique creates vectors of the units of text and then the most important units are extracted with the help of a semantic analysis technique (Maji & Fizi-Derakhshi, 2015).

A neural-network based application of the Memansa principle is used by Sakhare and Kumar (2016). Although they use it for English through neural nets, the approach for information extraction is taken from Mimamsa which makes it relevant to our discussion.

A pointer-generator method based on pre-trained word-embedding for ATS has been performed for English by Anh & Trang (2019). The application for Sanskrit will need to be tested though they had the prepared CNN/Dailymail dataset for training already. Another effort in IL ATS has been by Talukder et al. (2019) where the model used is sequence to sequence RNN. They report the loss of training error to 0.008.

The text-based method is classified as the third method. This is the corpus-based method deployed by others (Hasler et al, 2003; Edmundson, 1969) discussed in the next section.

Apart from graph-based methods, POS-NER based methods have also been deployed. Embar et al (2013) presents sArAmsha, an abstractive summarizer for Kannada. According to them, tools like POS tagging and NER implementation are used in the initial processing of documents and then an abstraction scheme is applied. This may also be classified under the corpus based approach.

3.1.3. Corpus based approach:

Under this, Corpus is annotated with relevant annotation schemes like POS, NER, discourse annotation tools like the Rhetorical-Structure Theory (Mann & Thompson, 1988; Jones, 1999; Zahri et al., 2015) etc, which helps in extracting meaning at a later stage.

Corpus type has also been used as an important basis for developing TS (Hasler et al., 2003). Annotation of corpora to indicate meaningful units in a text is a viable method. The works suggest that semantic abstraction becomes easier with this annotated corpora. However, Oya T. et al. (2014) use template-based abstractive summarization which they report has reduced dependence on annotated corpora.

3.1.4.

At this point, it is important to mention the extraction-based abstraction approach to TS one of which is the Information Extraction(IE) ATS (Kallimani et al, 2011). IE techniques are deployed in the initial stages in order to identify the important word units in the document. Abstraction is done from these extracted units (Kallimani et al, 2011; Afantenos et al., 2005).

Edmundson(1969) used a proper corpus divided into training and testing for summarization and evaluation. The method used is feature based only and he suggested that it was important to consider syntactic and semantic features in summarization. It may be noted that the 'abstracting' referred to in his article is focused on generating abstracts of articles based on extracted sentences. He terms this process as 'abstracting' (Edmundson & Wylls, 1961), though it is different from abstraction as we know it today.

Other than ATS, some prominent works in ETS for Indian Languages have been covered by Dhanya & Jathavedan (2013). The latter includes the thematic and positional score based method for Bengali (Sarkar, 2012); statistical features like cue phrase, title keyword, and similar features based extraction method for Punjabi (Gupta & Lehal, 2011); the graph- based text ranking method for Tamil (Sankar et al, 2011) performs extractive summary without any annotated corpora or supervised learning method.

Patel et al. (2007) and D'Silva & Sharma (2019) look at multilingual translation problems with language independent TS being one option (Patel et al., 2007). There are two reasons why it may not be useful to us. First, their approach is statistical and not semantic. It has been suggested by Edmundson (1969) that syntactic and semantic factors as well as context of a text (Jones, 1999) in TS be considered for better quality. We too believe that semantic representation is important for ATS. Two, their approach is mostly extractive. The other option, that of cross lingual TS using Machine Translation (MT) (D'Silva & Sharma, 2019) is a good option to be explored.

3.1.5.

A key point to be observed in these and general text summarization tools is the type and source of data. There are two primary domains of data on which most tools are based: Scientific articles and newspaper articles. Tools for the summary of these two types of texts are usually developed more. While extractive is a dominant approach for these domains, abstractive has also a good presence.

However, to begin a process in Sanskrit ATS, we have focused our study on contemporary prose consisting of mainly newspaper articles and Sanskrit blogs.

Observations regarding methods:

1. Scholars use TS methods in a mixed manner. For e.g., a semantic graph may require ontology deployment for better semantic representation (Moawad & Aref, 2012); abstractive summarizer may first extract relevant information before applying abstraction (Kalimanni et al, 2011).

2. Supervised methods will need label summaries along with the texts. Thus, newspaper articles with their headlines are usually taken as the standard training corpus where the headline serves as the summary of the respective text. This is a feasible approach for a beginner-level work.

4. Sanskrit ATS

Some features of the Sanskrit writings and their challenges can be stated as following:

- Sanskrit prose is strictly based on the principles of grammar which inspires its word-formation and usage. Owing to the Paninian model of Grammar, the language is rich in morphology. The principle of economy and precision have been important for Sanskrit prose(Kiparsky, 1991). As a result, while the prose in Sanskrit in general is appreciated for its economy, it becomes difficult for any man/machine processing, and more so for the ATS.

- **Compounds and Sandhis**: Sanskrit prose is constituted on the samhita (continuous text) principle thereby using Compounds and Sandhis (euphonic combination) heavily. For instance, multiple words combined after removing their inflections is an example of a compound. Space does not act as a delimiter largely here. This along with potentially recursive sandhi and complex morphology make preprocessing a critical task for Sanskrit texts.

- **Word Significance**: Most Sanskrit literary works, especially poetry, tend to be indirect in their intended meanings - abhidha(literal), lakshana(metaphor), vyanjana(euphemism). Poetry usually expresses meanings more than one but the same can go for most prose creations in literature also. The availability of lexical resources like the Amarakosha bear testimony to this fact, so does the long tradition of language analysis including the philosophy of Mimamsa (interpretation) and Nyaya (logic).

- **Diversity of verb usage**: While lakaras (tense) are used to denote time, some suffixes are also used to indicate past and present tense. Thus, for the same verb, different forms of it can be used to suggest the same meaning. For each such usage, meaning will have to be considered well before generating a summary of any type.

5. Preliminary Study

To perform a preliminary data study, a total of 1310 sentences have been extracted from online sources and stored as data files. Current prose like the news articles from the All India Radio, DD News and other sources have been considered at this stage. The following may be observed about the data:

1. Sentences are usually short, with not more than 7 words per sentence on an average.

2. Owing to the fact that most digital sources in Sanskrit found so far exist as a way to teach prospective learners, there is no variety in content found there.

3. News articles offer a good standard of sentences in Sanskrit while at the same time reducing the complexity of verbs. There are a few standard usages which ensure ease of meaning comprehension.

The short length of sentences indicates that with some basic preprocessing only, a TS method may be applied on the text. After going through the preliminary data, this has led us to conclude that we may start our work with focus on two approaches: first, a graph-based method. Owing to short sentences in the current prose, generating a graph and the prospective relations among words may be quicker and efficient.

Second, supervised method where news articles and their headlines are taken as corpora for training. This would be on the lines of the ATS developed on English and other languages using the CNN/Dailymail dataset (Mishra & Gayen, 2018).

Preprocessing of the text is a necessary stage in the approach (Barve et. al, 2015). This would ensure creation of words for ease of processing the text further. Contemporary simple prose that contains direct meanings instead of oblique ones should be used like Barve et al (2015) use Sanskrit Wikipedia articles to test their approaches (VSM, Graph and tf-isf).

A work on these two methods will suggest further course of action. Annotation may be required if the results so indicate.

6. Conclusion

This paper presents a preliminary attempt to develop a Sanskrit abstractive text summarizer for current prose. It surveyed the top abstractive summarization approaches to Indian languages, in general, with a view to zeroing in on one approach for the current work on Sanskrit ATS. Since there has not been any attempt at Sanskrit ATS so far, a beginning is being made for current Sanskrit prose mostly news articles. While summarization would not suit literary poetry, we could utilize dependency parsers to build semantic graphs for any verse in scientific texts. Prose in these texts could be further summarized if this work is advanced further from current prose to other prose styles. After surveying the available literature for ATS in ILs the authors propose that semantic approach would be better suited for the inherent complexities that Sanskrit is known for. Owing to rich morphology of the language, pre-defined structures may not result in a coherent or usable summary. Thus, a semantic approach would assist in arriving at a better analyzed summary. In the semantic approach, a graph-based method shall be a good start. Secondly, a supervised method for the available prose from the news article-headline combine may be emulated for Sanskrit too.

The possibility of annotation should be considered after this, if required.

The language of the output summary is one dimension of SATS which is out of the scope of this paper. For any other language, the abstracted summary is produced in the same language as the text. However, it could be explored if the abstractions of Sanskrit prose could be carried out in both Sanskrit as well as Hindi or English with the help of an existing Machine Translation.

7. References

Afantenos, S., Karkaletsis, V. & Stamatopoulos, P. (2005). Summarization from Medical Documents: A Survey. Artificial Intelligence in Medicine. 33. 157-177. 10.1016/j.artmed.2004.07.017.

Anh, D. T., & Trang, N. T. T. (2019, December). Abstractive Text Summarization Using Pointer-Generator Networks With Pre-trained Word Embedding. In *Proceedings of the Tenth International Symposium on Information and Communication Technology* (pp. 473-478).

Barve, S, Desai, S. & Sardinha, R. (2015). "Query-Based Extractive Text Summarization for Sanskrit". In: *Proceedings of the Fourth International Conference on Frontiers in Intelligent Computing: Theory and Applications(FICTA).* Springer. Digital Object I: 10.1007/978-81-322-2695-6_47

C. Sunitha, A., Jaya, & Ganesh, A. (2016). "A Study on Abstractive Summarization Techniques in Indian Languages". In: *Proceedings of the Fourth International Conference on Recent Trends in Computer Science and Engineering.* Procedia Computer Science. 87(2016). pp 25-31. Elsevier: DOI: 10.1016/j.procs.2016.05.121

D'Silva, J. & Sharma, U (2019). Automatic Text Summarization of Indian Languages: A Multilingual Problem. *Journal of Theoretical and Applied Information Technology. 97(11).*

Embar, V., Deshpande, S., Vaishnavi, A.K. & Jain, V. & Kallimani, J. (2013). sArAmsha - A Kannada abstractive summarizer. In: *Proceedings of the 2013 International Conference on Advances in Computing, Communications and Informatics, ICACCI* 2013. 540-544. 10.1109/ICACCI.2013.6637229.

Edmundson, H. P. (1969). New methods in automatic extracting. *Journal of the ACM (JACM), 16*(2), 264-285.

Edmundson, H. P., & Wyllys, R. E. (1961). Automatic abstracting and indexing—survey and recommendations. *Communications of the ACM, 4*(5), 226-234.

Gupta, V., & Lehal, G.S. (2011). Features Selection and Weight learning for Punjabi Text Summarization. *International Journal of Engineering Trends and Technology. 2(2).*

Giuseppe C & Jackie C. K. (2008), Extractive vs. NLG-based Abstractive Summarization of Evaluative Text: The Effect of Corpus Controversiality, *Proceedings of the Fifth International Natural Language Generation Conference, ACL,* https://www.aclweb.org/anthology/W08-1106

Hasler, L., Orasan, C., & Mitkov, R. (2003). Building better corpora for summarization. In *Proceedings of Corpus Linguistics* (pp. 309-319).

Hipola, P., Senso, J.A., Mederos-Leiva, A. & Dominguez-Velasco, S. (2014). Ontology-based text summarization. The case of Texminer. *Library HiTech. 32(2).* pp 229-248. Emerald. DOI: 10.1108/LHT-01-2014-0005.

Jones, K. S. (1999). Automatic summarizing: factors and directions. In Mani & Maybury (eds.) *Advances in automatic text summarization* (No. 1, pp. 1-12). Cambridge, Mass, USA: MIT press.

Kallimani, J. S., & Srinivasa, K. G. (2011). Information extraction by an abstractive text summarization for an Indian regional language. In *2011 7th International Conference on Natural Language Processing and Knowledge Engineering* (pp. 319-322). IEEE.

Kabeer, R. & Idicula, S. M.(2014). "Text summarization for Malayalam documents - An experience" In: *Proceedings of the International Conference on Data Science & Engineering* (ICDSE), Kochi, pp. 145-150.

Kiparsky, P. (1991). Economy and the Construction of Sivasutras. PDF.

Luhn, H. P. (1958). The automatic creation of literature abstracts. *IBM Journal of research and development, 2*(2), 159-165..

Mani, I. & Maybury, M. T. (1999). *Advances in Automatic Summarization.* MIT Press.

Mann, W. C., & Thompson, S. A. (1988). Rhetorical structure theory: Toward a functional theory of text organization. *Text-interdisciplinary Journal for the Study of Discourse, 8*(3). pp. 243-281.

Moawad, I F & Aref. M. (2012). "Semantic Graph Reduction Approach for Abstractive Text Summarization". In: *ICCES.* p 132-138. DOI: 10.1109/ICCES.2012.6408498

Mishra, R. and Gayen, T. (2018). "Automatic Lossless Summarization of News Articles with Abstract Meaning Representation." In: *Proceedings of the 3rd International Conference Computer Science and Computational Engineering.* Procedia Computer Science. PDF.

Oya, T., Mehdad, Y., Carenini, G., & Ng, R. (2014). A template-based abstractive meeting summarization: Leveraging summary and source text relationships. In *Proceedings of the 8th International Natural Language Generation Conference (INLG):* pp. 45-53.

Patel, A., Siddiqui, T., & Tiwary, U. S. (2007). A language independent approach to multilingual text summarization. *Large scale semantic access to content (text, image, video, and sound),* 123-132.

P.M, Dhanya & Jathavedan M. (2013). "Comparative Study of Text Summarization in Indian Languages." In: *International Journal of Computer Applications.* 75(6) : pp 17-21.

Ramezani, M. & Feizi-Derakhshi, Md. R. (2015). Ontology-Based Automatic Text Summarization using FarsNet. *Advances in Computer Science: an International Journal.* 4(2) no.14.

Russell, S J. & Norvig, P. (2019). *Artificial Intelligence: A Modern Approach.* Pearson.

Sankar, K., R, Vijay Sundar Kumar, Devi, S.L. (2011). Text Extraction for an Agglutinative Language. *Language in India. 11(5). Special Vol: Problem of Parsing in Indian languages.*

Sakhare, D.Y. and Kumar R (2016). Syntactical Knowledge and Sanskrit Memansa Principle Based Approach for Text Summarization" In: *International Journal of Computer Science and Information Security (IJCSIS).* 14(4). pp. 270-275. ISSN: 1947-5500.

Sarkar, K. (2012). Bengali text summarization by sentence extraction. *arXiv preprint arXiv:1201.2240.*

Subramaniam, M. & Dalal V. (2015). "Test Model for Rich Semantic Graph Representation for Hindi Text using Abstractive Method" In: *International Research Journal of Engineering and Technology.* 2(2). pp 113-116. e-ISSN:2395-0056

Talukder, M. A. I., Abujar S., Masum, A. K. M., Faisal, F. & Hossain, S. A. (2019). "Bengali abstractive text summarization using sequence to sequence RNNs," *10th International Conference on Computing, Communication and Networking Technologies (ICCCNT).* pp. 1-5.

Zahri, N.A.H., Fukumoto, F., Suguru, M., & Lynn, O.B. (2015). Applications of Rhetorical Relations Between Sentences to Cluster-Based Text Summarization. in Nagamalai et al. (eds.) *CCSEA, DKMP, AIFU,* SEA-2015. pp. 73-92. 10.5121/csit.2015.50207.

Proceedings of the WILDRE5– 5th Workshop on Indian Language Data: Resources and Evaluation, pages 66–72
Language Resources and Evaluation Conference (LREC 2020), Marseille, 11–16 May 2020
© European Language Resources Association (ELRA), licensed under CC-BY-NC

A Deeper Study on Features for Named Entity Recognition

Malarkodi C. S. and Sobha Lalitha Devi
AU-KBC Research Centre
MIT Campus of Anna University
Chromepet, Chennai, India
sobha@au-kbc.org

Abstract

This paper deals with the various features used for the identification of named entities. The performance of the machine learning system heavily depends on the feature selection criteria. The intention to trace the essential features required for the development of named entity system across languages motivated us to conduct this study. The linguistic analysis was done to find out the part of speech patterns surrounding the context of named entities and from the observation linguistic oriented features are identified for both Indian and European languages. The Indian languages belongs to Dravidian language family such as Tamil, Telugu, Malayalam, Indo-Aryan language family such as Hindi, Punjabi, Bengali and Marathi, European languages such as English, Spanish, Dutch, German and Hungarian are used in this work. The machine learning technique CRFs was used for the system development. The experiments were conducted using the linguistic features and the results obtained for each languages are comparable with state-of-art systems.

Keywords: features, ner, CRFs, POS patterns, named entities

1. Related Work

Named Entity Recognition (NER) is defined as the process of automatic identification of proper nouns and classifies the identified entities into predefined categories such as person, location, organization, facilities, products, temporal or numeric expressions etc. Even though named entity recognition is a well-established research filed and lot of research works are available for various languages, to the best of our language no work was found on the deeper analysis of features required for named entity system across languages.

Initially the term NER was defined in Message Understanding Conference (MUC), when the structured information about company and defense related activities needed to be extracted from the unstructured text. It was noticed that the main information units to be extracted are named entities (Grishman et al. 1996). The very first research work in NER was done by Lisa F. Rau, who developed the system to recognize company names using hand-crafted rules. In MUC-7, five out of eight systems were generated using rule based method (Chinchor 1998). Nadeau et al. (2007) has reported fifteen years of research carried out in the field of entity recognition.

Gutiérrez et al. (2015) developed a Spanish NE system using CRF. The dataset was obtained from CONLL 2002 shared task. Ekbal et al. (2008) worked on a Bengali named entity recognition using CRF. Ekbal et al. (2009) contributed NER systems for Hindi & Bengali using CRF framework. Kaur et al. (2012) built an NE system for Punjabi language. Bindu & Sumam Mary (2012) used CRF based approach for identifying named entities in Malayalam text.

Khanam et.al. (2016) has worked on the Named Entity Identification for Telugu Language using hybrid approach. Sobha et al. (2007) developed a multilingual named entity system to identify the place names using Finite State Automaton (FSA). Vijayakrishna & Sobha (2008) focused on the Tamil NER for tourism domain which consists of nested tagging of named entities. Malarkodi & Sobha (2012a) built a NE system for Indian languages like Tamil, Telugu, Hindi, Marathi, Punjabi and Bengali using CRF. Malarkodi et al. (2012b) discussed the various challenges,

while developing the NE system in Tamil language. Sobha et al. (2013) has participated in ICON NLP tool contest and submitted the test runs for 5 Indian languages and English.

Patil et al. (2016) reported a work on NER for Marathi using HMM. Jaspreet et al. (2015) contributed Punjabi NER using 2 machine learning approaches namely HMM and MEMM. Antony et.al. (2014) constructed the NE system for Tamil Biomedical documents using SVM classifier. Lakshmi et.al. (2016) has worked on the Malayalam NER using Fuzzy-SVM and it is based on the semantic features and linguistic grammar rules. Jiljo et.al. (2016) used TnT and Maximum Entropy Markov model for NE identification in Malayalam data. The proposed methodology yields 82.5% accuracy.

Bojórquez et al. (2015) worked on improving the Spanish NER used in the Text Dialog System (TDS) by using semi-supervised technique. Zea et.al. (2016) developed a semi-supervised NE system for Spanish language. Athavale et al. (2016) described a Neural Network model for NER based on the Bi Directional RNN-LSTM. In order to identify the mentions of medications, Adverse Drug Event (ADE) and symptoms of the diseases in the clinical notes (Florez et al. 2018) proposed the character-level word representation methods which can be used as an input feature to neural network model called LSTM.

The various shared tasks conducted for Named Entity Recognition are discussed in this section. In 2002, CONLL shared task about NER was focused on Spanish and Dutch (Tjong et al. 2002). The CONLL 2003 offered dataset for English and German (Tjong et al. 2003). The NERSSEAL shared task of IJCNLP-2008 was organized for 5 Indian Languages namely Hindi, Bengali, Oriya, Telugu and Urdu (Singh, 2008). In 2013 AU-KBC has organized NER shared task as part of Forum for Information Retrieval for Evaluation (FIRE), to create a benchmark data for Indian Languages. The dataset was released for 4 Indian Languages like Bengali, Hindi, Malayalam, and Tamil and also for English. The various techniques used by the participants are CRF, rule based approach and list based search (Pattabhi & Sobha 2013). The 2nd edition of NER track for IL has organized as part of FIRE 2014 for English and 3 IL namely Hindi, Malayalam, and Tamil. The main focus of this track is nested entity identification. The participants have used CRF and SVM for system development (Pattabhi et al. 2014).

2. Language Families Used

The Indian languages belong to different language families; most of the Indian languages come under Indo-Aryan and Dravidian language families. Indo Aryan language family is a sub-branch of Indo-Iranian family which itself is a sub-family of Indo-European language family. Mainly the Indian languages like Hindi, Bengali, Marathi, Punjabi comes under Indo-Aryan family and Indian languages like Tamil, Telugu, Malayalam, and Kannada belongs to a Dravidian language family. The European languages also have several language families. The languages like German, Dutch and English belong to Germanic families, Spanish language constitutes a Romance language family and Hungarian comes under Uralic language family.

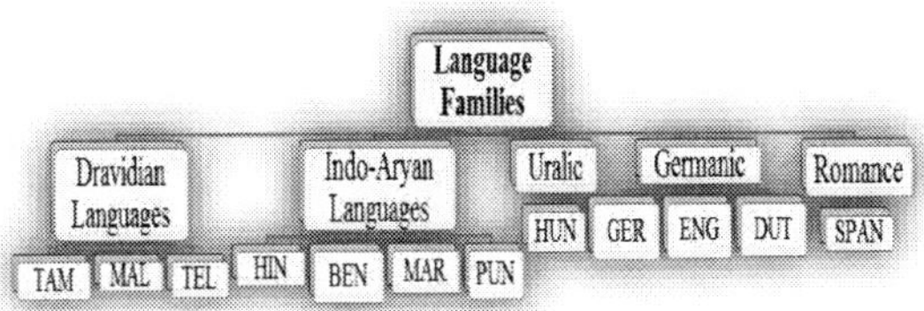

Figure 1 : Language Families Used in this work

3. Corpus Statistics

In this section, we discuss the corpus we have used for the study. The corpus for Tamil, Malayalam, and English was collected using an automated crawler program. The dataset developed as part of FIRE 2013 NER shared task and national level projects such as Cross Lingual Information Access (CLIA) are used for English, Tamil, Hindi, Malayalam, Bengali, Marathi and Punjabi. The corpus statistics of the Dravidian Languages are given in Table 1. The Tamil dataset consists of 13k sentences, 200K tokens and 27k named entities. The Malayalam corpus consists of 64,345 tokens, 5k sentences and 11k named entities. The Telugu corpus has 2K sentences, 43,062 tokens and 9,104 named entities.

Languages	Tokens	Sentences	NEs
Tamil	2,04,144	13,571	27,498
Telugu	43,062	2,150	9,104
Malayalam	64,345	5,107	11,380
Bengali	52,024	4,030	2,690
Hindi	1,90,236	14,098	21,498
Marathi	73,523	6,138	6,036

Table 1: Corpus statistics (Indian Languages)

The NE corpus used for Spanish and Dutch languages is obtained from CONLL 2003 NER shared task. The Spanish and Dutch corpus contains person, location, organization and miscellaneous NE tags. For German language, the GERMEVAL NER shared task data has been utilized. The German NE corpus has 12 NE tags and mainly has four classes. The number of tokens and named entities in the English dataset are 200K and 25K respectively. The Spanish and Dutch corpus consists of 300K and 200K tokens. The numbers of named entities in Spanish and Dutch dataset are 23,148 and 27,390. The German dataset consists of 500K tokens, 31K sentences and 33,399 NEs. The Hungarian corpus has 400K tokens and 7,068 named entities.

Languages	Tokens	Sentences	NEs
English	2,56,426	14,002	25,671
Dutch	2,47,820	15,316	27,390
Hungarian	4,44,661	27,673	7,068
German	5,91,005	31,298	33,399
Spanish	3,17,637	10,238	23,148

Table 2: Corpus statistics (European Languages)

The details of the POS tagset are explained in this section. The BIS POS tagset was used for Indian Languages. The Tamil POS tagger developed by Sobha et al. (2016) works with an accuracy of 95.16% (Sobha et al., 2016). The Brills POS tagger (Brill et al., 1992) is used for this task. The dataset used for German are preprocessed with Stanford POS tagger (Manning et al., 2014). The Spanish and Dutch dataset are obtained from the CONLL shared task are already tagged with POS information.

4. Features used for Named Entity Recognition

The part of speech patterns frequently occurred in the context of named entities are analyzed for each language and the results are discussed in this section. We analyze the corpus to arrive at the most suitable word level features for identifying the NE which can be used for machine learning purposes. We have taken a window of three words and identified the most frequent grammatical and typographical feature that occurs. The distribution of each feature in each language is given in detail below.

4.1 Analysis of common Linguistic features

In Tamil corpus, the named entities occurred at the beginning of the sentence in 3,776 instances and in 2,056 instances named entities occurred at the end of the sentence, punctuations preceded the NE in 6,222 times and 4,596 times punctuations succeed the NE, common nouns preceded the NE in 6,274 times and succeeded the NE in 9,038 times, proper nouns occurred before NE in 2,250 instances and after NE in 2,868 instances. The postpositions occurred before NE in 999 instances, adjectives occurred before NE in 1418 instances and conjunction occurred before NE in 384 times. The verbal participle preceding the named entities in 716 instances and the relative participle verbs preceded the NE in 1,007 times. The finite verbs succeed the NE in 998 instances, postpositions, adverb, and adjectives occurred at 1131, 980 and 878 instances respectively.

The Malayalam corpus has the following distribution. The named entities occurred at the beginning of the sentence in 1,062 instances and in 72 instances named entities occurred at the end of the sentence, punctuations preceded the NE in 818 times and 751 times punctuations succeed the NE, common nouns preceded the NE in 1,281 times and succeeded the NE in 1,794 times, proper nouns occurred before NE in 774 instances and after NE in 939 instances. The postpositions occurred before NE in 209 instances, adjectives occurred before NE in 201 instances and conjunction occurred before NE in 85 times. The verbal participle preceding the named entities in 82 instances and the relative participle verbs preceded the NE in 238 times. The finite verbs succeed the NE in 628 instances, postpositions, adverb, and adjectives occurred at 192, 173 and 273 instances respectively.

In Telugu corpus, the named entities occurred at the beginning of the sentence in 776 instances and in 17 instances named entities occurred at the end of the sentence, punctuations preceded the NE in 588 times and 610 times punctuations succeed the NE, common nouns preceded the NE in 3722 times and succeeded the NE in 4641 times, proper nouns occurred before NE in 540 instances and after NE in 615 instances. The postpositions occurred before NE in 450 instances, adjectives occurred before NE in 315 instances and conjunction occurred before NE in 153 times. The verbs preceding the named entities in 1541 instances and the relative participle verbs preceded the NE in 78 times. The verbs succeed the NE in 1307 instances, postpositions, adverb and adjectives occurred at 665, 263 and 256 instances respectively.

The Hindi corpus has the following distribution. The named entities occurred at the beginning of the sentence in 5,290 instances and in 1,201 instances named entities occurred at the end of the sentence, punctuations preceded the NE in 2281 times and 2070 times punctuations succeed the NE, common nouns preceded the NE in 1862 times and succeeded the NE in 1307 times, proper nouns occurred before NE in 1055 instances and after NE in 753 instances. The postpositions occurred before NE in 3536 instances, adjectives occurred before NE in 611 instances and conjunction occurred before NE in 1844 times. The verbs preceding the named entities in 349 instances and the relative participle verbs preceded the NE in 412 times. The verbs succeed the NE in 876 instances, postpositions, adverb and adjectives occurred at 915, 536 and 436 instances respectively.

In Punjabi corpus, the named entities occurred at the beginning of the sentence in 1267 instances and in 831 instances named entities occurred at the end of the sentence, punctuations preceded the NE in 499 times and 475 times punctuations succeed the NE, common nouns preceded the NE in 1,119 times and succeeded the NE in 684 times, proper nouns occurred before NE in 304 instances and after NE in 304 instances. The postpositions occurred before NE in 1363 instances, adjectives occurred before NE in 553 instances and conjunction occurred before NE in 227 times. The verbs preceding the named entities in 99 instances and the relative participle verbs preceded the NE in 176 times. The verbs succeed the NE in 361 instances, postpositions, adverb and adjectives occurred at 3,211, 136 and 158 instances respectively.

In Bengali corpus, the NE distribution is as discussed here. The named entities occurred at the beginning of the sentence in 630 instances and in 312 instances named entities occurred at the end of the sentence, punctuations preceded the NE in 288 times and 204 times punctuations succeed the NE, common nouns preceded the NE in 561 times and succeeded the NE in 908 times, proper nouns occurred before NE in 197 instances and after NE in 199 instances. The postpositions occurred before NE in 120 instances, adjectives occurred before NE in 148 instances and conjunction occurred before NE in 239 times. The verbs preceding the named entities in 208 instances and the relative participle verbs preceded the NE in 25 times. The verbs succeed the NE in 290 instances, postpositions, adverb and adjectives occurred at 159, 280 and 238 instances respectively.

The Marathi corpus has the following distribution. The named entities occurred at the beginning of the sentence is 967 instances and in 488 instances named entities occurred at the end of the sentence, punctuations preceded the NE in 609 times and 566 times punctuations succeed the NE, common nouns preceded the NE in 1956 times and succeeded the NE in 1879 times, proper nouns occurred before NE in 348 instances and after NE in 219 instances. The postpositions occurred before NE in 14 instances, adjectives occurred before NE in 114 instances and conjunction occurred before NE in 466 times. The verbs preceding the named entities in 475 instances and the relative participle verbs preceded the NE in 38 times. The verbs succeed the NE in 419 instances, postpositions, adverb and adjectives occurred at 212, 253 and 392 instances respectively.

In English corpus, the NE distribution is as discussed here. The named entities occurred at the beginning of the sentence in 1,014 instances and in 2,078 instances named entities occurred at the end of the sentence, punctuations preceded the NE in 1549 times and 2078 times punctuations succeed the NE, common nouns preceded the NE in 1239 times and succeeded the NE in 1289 times, proper nouns occurred before NE in 745 instances and after NE in 823 instances. The prepositions occurred before NE in 2794 instances. The determiners preceding the named entities in 1425 instances. The verbal participle preceding the named entities in 156 instances. The finite verbs succeed the NE in 680 instances, prepositions and conjunctions occurred at 1195 and 774 instances respectively.

The Spanish corpus has the following distribution. The named entities occurred at the beginning of the sentence in 2046 instances and in 2,131 instances named entities occurred at the end of the sentence, punctuations preceded the NE in 2404 times and 7010 times punctuations succeed the NE, nouns preceded the NE in 1123 times and succeeded the NE in 204 times. The prepositions occurred before NE in 7231 instances. The determiners preceding the named entities in 3993 instances. The verbs succeed the NE in 2060 instances, prepositions and conjunctions occurred at 2116 and 1648 instances respectively.

In Dutch corpus, the NE distribution is as discussed here. The named entities occurred at the beginning of the sentence in 5605 instances and in 2787 instances named entities occurred at the end of the sentence, punctuations preceded the NE in 4142 times and 10321 times punctuations succeed the NE, nouns preceded the NE in 2627 times and succeeded the NE in 3174 times. The prepositions occurred before NE in 5146 instances. The determiners preceding the named entities in 4142 instances. The verbs succeed the NE in 4657 instances, prepositions and conjunctions occurred at 2062 and 1411 instances respectively.

The German corpus has the following distribution. The named entities occurred at the beginning of the sentence in 2033 instances and in 128 instances named entities occurred at the end of the sentence, punctuations preceded the NE in 966 times and 2535 times punctuations succeed the NE, common nouns preceded the NE in 5012 times and succeeded the NE in 3886 times, proper nouns occurred before NE in 321 instances and after NE in 608 instances. The prepositions occurred before NE in 5869 instances. The determiners preceding the named entities in 7166 instances. The finite verbs succeed the NE in 3140 instances, prepositions and conjunctions occurred at 3075 and 2059 instances respectively.

In Hungarian corpus, the NE distribution is as discussed here. The named entities occurred at the beginning of the sentence is 2175 instances and in 26 instances named entities occurred at the end of the sentence, punctuations preceded the NE in 878 times and 1861 times punctuations succeed the NE, nouns preceded the NE in 845 times and succeeded the NE in 2053 times. The postpositions occurred before NE in 148 instances. The determiners preceding the named entities in 1788 instances. The finite verbs succeed the NE in 751 instances, prepositions and conjunctions occurred at 220 and 439 instances respectively.

We have analysed the corpus for the various part of speech which is associated with the named entities. In the window of three, the following are the grammatical features that occurred. Also, the Typographical features also arrive through the analysis. From the above analysis, we arrived at the following points

- ➢ In Dravidian languages Tamil, Telugu and Malayalam the most commonly occurring pattern for NE are
- ➢ Grammatical patterns
  - RP verbs precede and follow
  - Common noun precedes or follows
  - Occurring after the verb
  - Postpositions precede the NEs
  - Verbs succeed the NEs
  - Postpositions, adjectives or adverbs follow the NEs

- ➢ Typological patterns are
  - NEs at the beginning of the sentence
  - NEs at the end of the sentence
  - Punctuations followed NEs
  - NEs Occurring after punctuations

- ➢ In Indo Aryan Languages Hindi, Bengali, Marathi, and Punjabi the most commonly occurring pattern for NE are
  - The common nouns, pronouns or conjunctions precedes the NEs

- Verbs precede in Bengali and Marathi
- The postpositions precede the NEs in Hindi and Punjabi
- NEs following by postposition, verbs, conjunctions or adjectives
- Occurring at the beginning of the sentence.
- ➢ Typological patterns are
  - NEs at the beginning of the sentence
  - NEs at the end of the sentence
  - Punctuations followed NEs
  - NEs Occurring after punctuations
- ➢ In European Languages English, Hungarian, Spanish, Dutch, and German the most commonly occurring pattern for NE are
  - Follows by verbs, common nouns or punctuations
  - Prepositions, determiners or punctuations precedes
  - Verbs or adjectives precede the NEs in Hungarian, Dutch and German.
  - Occurring at the beginning of the sentence
- ➢ Typological patterns are
  - NEs at the beginning of the sentence
  - NEs at the end of the sentence
  - Punctuations followed NEs
  - NEs Occurring after punctuations

5. Experiments & Results

In this section, the results obtained by each feature combinations are discussed in detail. The experiments are conducted for each language is given in the table. The machine learning technique CRFs was used for the system development.

Languages	PRE	REC	F-M
Tamil	80.12	83.1	81.58
Malayalam	70.63	74.82	72.66
Telugu	69.4	57.25	62.74

Table 3: Results for Dravidian Languages

Languages	PRE	REC	F-M
Hindi	81.05	83.13	82.07
Bengali	82.78	89.31	85.92
Punjabi	80.54	83.45	81.96
Marathi	78.32	87.32	82.57

Table 4: Results for Indo-Aryan Languages

Languages	PRE	REC	F-M
English	84.32	80.35	82.28
Spanish	86.13	84.37	85.24
Dutch	90.3	92.23	91.25
Hungarian	83.84	85.21	84.51
German	81.41	72.99	76.97

Table 5: Results for European Languages

The linguistic feature yielded the precision and recall of 80.12% and 83.1% for Tamil, 70.63% precision and 74.82% recall for Malayalam and 69.40% precision score and 57.25% recall value for Telugu. The f-score obtained by Dravidian languages are 81% for Tamil, 72% for Malayalam and 62.74% in Telugu.

The results obtained Indo-Aryan languages using linguistic feature are discussed in this section. The precision and recall achieved for Hindi is 80.12% and 83.1% respectively. Bengali has obtained the f-score of 85%. Punjabi scored the precision of 80.54% and recall of 83.45%. Marathi has achieved the f- measure of 82.57%.

The results obtained European languages using linguistic feature are discussed in this section. The precision and recall achieved for English is 84% and 80% respectively. Spanish has obtained the f-score of 85%. Dutch scored the precision of 90.3% and recall of 92.23%. Hungarian has achieved the f- measure of 84.57%. German has obtained the precision of 81%, recall of 72% and f-measure of 76% respectively.

The different feature combinations shown in Table 3-5 clearly show that all the linguistic features used in the present system have the capability to improve the system's performance. The results show that the feature combinations presented in this work yields reasonable results not only for Indian Languages but also for European languages. By using linguistic features alone, we have achieved reasonable scores for languages belong to different language families.

Existing Systems	Methods	Languages used	F-M
Gayen et al. (2014)	HMM	Bengali	85.99
		English	77.04
		Hindi	75.20
		Marathi	42.89
		Punjabi	54.55
		Tamil	44.00
		Telugu	40.03
Abinaya et al. (2014)	CRF for English SVM for other languages	English	57.81
		Hindi	25.53
		Tamil	30.75
		Malayalam	24.91
Ekbal et al. (2009)	CRF	Bengali (LI)	77.74
		Hindi (LI)	77.08
Florian et al. (2003)	Stacking based approach	Spanish	79.05
		Dutch	74.99
Our system	CRFs	Bengali	85.92
		Hindi	82.07
		Marathi	82.57
		Punjabi	81.96
		Tamil	81.58
		Telugu	62.74
		Malayalam	72.66
		English	82.28
		Spanish	85.24
		Dutch	91.25
		German	76.97
		Hungarian	84.51

Table 6: Comparison with existing works

Though the present work is about multilingual named entities, we have compared our work with the existing multilingual NER works. Gayen et al. (2014) has participated in ICON NER shared task and built a named entity system for English and 6 Indian languages using HMM. In comparison with the performance reported by Gayen et al. (2014), except Bengali we have achieved the highest f-score for all the Indian languages. Abinaya et al. (2014) has participated in FIRE 2014 shared task and developed a NE system for English and 3 Indian Languages. As reported in FIRE 2014 NER task overview paper (Pattabhi et al., 2014), the results given in table 6 are obtained by Abinaya et al. for maximal entities. They have implemented CRFs for English and SVM for other languages. The present system achieved the better scores than Abinaya et al. The language Independent (LI) NE system has developed for Hindi and Bengali using CRFs by Ekbal et al. (2009). The results attained by the present work in Bengali and Hindi languages are higher than Ekbal et al. (2009). But the NE system developed using language specific features by Ekbal et al. (2009) are performing better than the present system. Florian et al. (2003) participated in CONLL 2002 NER shared task and obtained 79.05% for Spanish and 74.99% for Dutch. The present system obtained 85% and 91% f-measure for Spanish and Dutch respectively.

6. Conclusion

The different kinds of features used for the named entity recognition are discussed in this work. The linguistic analysis of POS patterns precedes and following the named entities are analyzed for each language and from the observation linguistic features for the POS patterns are identified in the proximity of NE. This helps the system to learn the structure of named entities by providing the linguistic information. The experiments are conducted for both Indian and European languages. The results shown that the linguistic features obtained state-of-art results for both Indian and European languages.

7. Bibliographical References

Abinaya, N. Neethu, J. Barathi, H.B.G. Anand, M.K. & Soman, K.P. (2014). AMRITA CEN@ FIRE-2014: Named Entity Recognition for Indian Languages using Rich Features. In Proceedings of the Forum for Information Retrieval Evaluation, pp. 103-111

Antony, J.B. & Mahalakshmi, G.S. (2014). Named entity recognition for Tamil biomedical documents. In Proceedings of the 2014 International Conference on Circuits, Power and Computing Technologies, ICCPCT-2014, pp. 1571-1577.

Athavale, V. Bharadwaj, S., Pamecha, M., Prabhu, A. & Shrivastava, M. (2016). Towards deep learning in hindi ner: An approach to tackle the labelled data scarcity. arXiv preprint arXiv:1610.09756.

Brill, Eric. (1992). A simple rule-based part of speech tagger. In Proceedings of the third conference on Applied natural language processing. Association for Computational Linguistics.

Bojórquez, Salvador, S. & Victor, M.G. (2015). Semi-Supervised Approach to Named Entity Recognition in Spanish Applied to a Real-World Conversational System. Pattern Recognition: 7th Mexican Conference, MCPR 2015, Mexico City, Mexico, vol. 9116, pp. 24-27.

Chinchor, N. (1998). Overview of MUC 7. In Proceedings of the Seventh Message Understanding Conference (MUC-7), Fairfax, Virginia.

Ekbal, A. & Bandyopadhyay, S. (2008). Bengali named entity recognition using support vector machine. In Proceedings of the IJCNLP-08 Workshop on Named Entity Recognition for South and South East Asian Languages.

Ekbal, A. & Bandyopadhyay, S. (2009). A Conditional Random Field Approach for Named Entity Recognition in Bengali and Hindi. Linguistic Issues in Language Technology, Vol. 2, no. 1, 1-44.

Florez, E., Precioso, F., Riveill, M. & Pighetti, R. (2018). Named entity recognition using neural networks for clinical notes. International Workshop on Medication and Adverse Drug Event Detection, pp. 7-15.

Florian, R. Ittycheriah, A. Jing, H. & Zhang, T. (2003). Named entity recognition through classifier combination. In Proceedings of the seventh conference on Natural language learning at HLT-NAACL 2003. Association for Computational Linguistics, vol. 4, pp. 168-171

Gayen, V. & Sarkar, K. (2014). An HMM based named entity recognition system for Indian languages: the JU system at ICON 2013. ICON NLP Tool Contest arXiv preprint arXiv:1405.7397

Grishman, R & Beth, S. (1996). Message understanding conference-6: A brief history. In Proceedings of the16th International Conference on Computational Linguistics, Vol. 1

Gutiérrez, R., Castillo, A., Bucheli, V., & Solarte, O. (2015). Named Entity Recognition for Spanish language and applications in technology forecasting Reconocimiento de entidades nombradas para el idioma Español y su aplicación en la vigilancia tecnológica. Rev. Antioqueña las Ciencias Comput. y la Ing Softw, 5, 43-47.

Jaspreet, S. & Gurpreet, S.L. (2015). Named entity recognition for Punjabi language using Hmm and Memm. In Proceedings of the IRF International Conference, Pune, India, pp. 4-7.

Jiljo, Pranav, P.V. (2016). A study on named entity recognition for malayalam language using tnt tagger & maximum entropy markov model. International Journal of Applied Engineering Research, 11(8), pp. 5425-5429.

Kaur, A. & Josan, G.S. (2015). Evaluation of Named Entity Features for Punjabi Language. Procedia Computer Science 46, 159-166.

Bindu, M.S. & Idicula, S.M. (2011). Named entity identifier for malayalam using linguistic principles employing statistical methods. International Journal of Computer Science Issues (IJCSI), 8(5), 185.

Khanam, M.H. Khudhus, M.A. & Babu, M.P. (2016). Named entity recognition using machine learning techniques for Telugu language. In Proceedings of the 7th IEEE International Conference on Software Engineering and Service Science (ICSESS), pp. 940-944.

Lakshmi, G. Janu, R.P. & Meera, M. (2016). Named entity recognition in Malayalam using fuzzy support vector machine. In Proceedings of the 2016 International Conference on Information Science (ICIS), IEEE, pp. 201-206.

Malarkodi, C.S., Pattabhi, R.K. & Sobha L. (2012). Tamil NER–Coping with Real Time Challenges. In Proceedings of the Workshop on Machine Translation and Parsing in Indian Languages(MTPIL-2012), COLING, pp. 23-38.

Malarkodi, C.S & Sobha L (2012). A Deeper Look into Features for NE Resolution in Indian Languages. In Proceedings of the Workshop on Indian Language Data: Resources and Evaluation, LREC, Istanbul, pp. 36-41.

Manning, C, Surdeanu, M, Bauer, J, Finkel, J, Bethard, S & McClosky, D 2014, 'The Stanford CoreNLP natural language processing toolkit', Proceedings of 52nd annual meeting of the association for computational linguistics: system demonstrations, pp. 55-60

Nadeau, D. & Sekine, S. (2007). A survey of named entity recognition and classification. Linguisticae Investigationes, Vol. 30, no. 1, pp. 3–26.

Patil, N., Patil, A.S. & Pawar, B.V. (2016). Issues and Challenges in Marathi Named Entity Recognition. International Journal on Natural Language Computing (IJNLC), Vol. 5, pp. 15-30.

Pattabhi, R.K. & Sobha, L. (2013). NERIL: Named Entity Recognition for Indian Languages @ FIRE 2013–An Overview. FIRE-2013.

Pattabhi, R.K., Malarkodi C.S., Ram V.S. & Sobha L. (2014). NERIL: Named Entity Recognition for Indian Languages @ FIRE 2014–An Overview. FIRE-2014.

Singh, A.K. (2008). Named Entity Recognition for South and South East Asian Languages: Taking Stock. In Proceedings of the IJCNLP-08, pp. 5-16.

Sobha L, Malarkodi, C.S, & Marimuthu, K. (2013). Named Entity Recognizer for Indian Languages. ICON NLP Tool Contest.

Sobha, L. Pattabhi RK Rao, & Vijay Sundar Ram, R (2016). AUKBC Tamil Part-of-Speech Tagger (AUKBC-TamilPoSTagger 2016v1). Web Download. Computational Linguistics Research Group, AU-KBC Research Centre, Chennai, India.

Tjong Kim Sang, E.F. (2002). Introduction to the CoNLL-2002 shared task: Language-independent named entity recognition. In Proceedings of the CONLL-2002, Taipei, Taiwan.

Tjong Kim Sang, E.F & De Meulder, F. (2003). Introduction to the CoNLL-2003 shared task: Language-independent named entity recognition. In Proceedings of the seventh conference on Natural language learning at HLT-NAACL 2003, Vol. 4, pp. 142-147.

Vijayakrishna, R & Sobha, L. (2008). Domain focused Named Entity for Tamil using Conditional Random Fields. In Proceedings of the workshop on NER for South and South East Asian Languages, Hyderabad, India, pp. 59-66.

Zea, J.L.C., Luna, J.E.O., Thorne, C. & Glavaš, G. (2016). Spanish ner with word representations and conditional random fields'. In Proceedings of the sixth named entity workshop, pp. 34-40.